# STUDIES IN PHILOSOPHY

JOHN M. HEATON

1925–2017

edited by
Robert Nozick
*Pellegrino University Professor*
*at Harvard University*

*A GARLAND SERIES*

# Logic and Language in Wittgenstein's *Tractatus*

Ian Proops

Garland Publishing, Inc.
New York & London/2000

Published in 2000 by
Garland Publishing, Inc.
29 West 35th Street
New York, NY 10001

*Garland is an imprint of the Taylor & Francis group*

10  9  8  7  6  5  4  3  2  1

*Library of Congress Cataloging-in-Publication Data*
Proops, Ian.
 Logic and language in Wittgenstein's Tractatus / Ian Proops.
  p. cm. — (Studies in philosophy)
 Includes bibliographical references and index.
 ISBN 0-8153-3793-0 (alk. paper)
  1. Wittgenstein, Ludwig, 1889-1951. Tractatus logico-philosophicus. 2. Language and logic. I. Title. II. Studies in philosophy (New York, N.Y.)
 B3376.W563 T7367 2000
 192—dc21
                                                    00-026427

Printed on acid-free, 250 year-life paper
Manufactured in the United States of America

# Contents

# Preface

This work is a minimally revised version of my Harvard doctoral thesis, which was written during the years 1994–1998. My understanding of Wittgenstein's early philosophy has of course continued to evolve since completing the thesis, but because the attempt to incorporate these new ideas seemed likely to result in a wholly new work, I have decided to present the dissertation in its original form, with the exception of a few minor and mostly stylistic changes.

Two publications derive from the thesis. "The Early Wittgenstein on Logical Assertion" (*Philosophical Topics*, vol. 25, no. 2. fall 1997) and "The *Tractatus* on Inference and Entailment" (Forthcoming in Erich Reck, ed., *From Frege to Wittgenstein: Essays on Early Analytic Philosophy* (OUP)). The former closely follows chapter II, while the latter is a distant cousin of chapter IV. I am grateful to Erich Reck and Christopher Hill for permission to use material from these articles in this edition.

INP
Ann Arbor, MI
August, 1999

# Acknowledgments

I should like to thank my dissertation advisors: Warren Goldfarb, Richard Heck and Charles Parsons, for their wise and friendly guidance during the preparation of this thesis. I am deeply grateful for the interest they have shown in my work, and for the considerable energy and time they have devoted to improving it. Naturally, their influence on this thesis has been pervasive: so much so, that it would be safest to assume it present throughout.

Four philosophers outside the committee—Steven Gross, Peter Sullivan, Jamie Tappenden and Michael Potter—read all, or most, of the dissertation. I am grateful to them for their comments and encouragement at key stages in the writing of the dissertation. I owe special thanks to Steven for his services as interlocutor-of-first-resort, and to Peter Sullivan for his encouragement at early stages of my philosophical career.

It has been my good fortune to have been able to work with many distinguished philosophers in the Boston area. My understanding of the analytic tradition has benefited enormously from seminars by the late Burton Dreben at Boston University, and from lectures and seminars by Richard Cartwright and the late George Boolos at MIT.

For detailed comments on various chapters I owe thanks to: Thomas Ricketts, Ori Simchen, Juliet Floyd, Markus Stepanians, Sanford Shieh, Oystein Linnebo, Michael Glanzberg, Ed Holland, Hugh Miller and Adam Leite; and for philosophical conversation to: Jim Pryor, Gisela Striker, Peter Railton, Alison Simmons, Sean Greenberg, John Carriero, Sally Sedgwick, Josh Green, Scott

Shuchart, David Macarthur, Jason Stanley, Zoltán Szabó, Leif Wenar, Åsa Wikforss, Stephan Gutzeit, Tom Kelly and Dirk Lumma.

I am grateful to the R. M. Martin Fellowship of the Philosophy Department of Harvard University and the Harvard Graduate Society for their invaluable financial support. My years in graduate school were made considerably easier by the administrative assistance of Elizabeth McIsaac and Ghanda DiFiglia. I thank them both.

I wish to thank Sadia Abbas for her patience, irony and sense of the absurd, and for her sustained—and sustaining—good humour during the final stages of the project. But I have one debt of gratitude that surpasses all others. It is to my father, Jim Proops, for his years of support and encouragement. The dissertation is dedicated to him—with gratitude and love.

# Abbreviations

| | |
|---|---|
| *Begriffsschrift*: | G. Frege, *Begriffsschrift, eine der arithmetischen nachgebildete Formelsprache des reinen Denkens* (Halle: Louis Nebert, 1879). (English translation in van Heijenoort (1967)). |
| *Collected Papers*: | G. Frege, *Collected Papers*, ed. Brian McGuinness, trans. Hans Kaal et. al. (Oxford: Blackwell, 1980). |
| *CP Vol. II*: | B. Russell, *Philosophical Papers 1896-99, The Collected Papers of Bertrand Russell, Vol II*, Edited by Nicholas Griffin, Albert C. Lewis, and William C. Stratton (London: Routledge, 1990). |
| *CP Vol. III*: | B. Russell, *Toward the "Principles of Mathematics," The Collected Papers of Bertrand Russell, Vol. III*, Gregory H. Moore, ed. (London: Routledge, 1993). |
| *CP Vol. IV*: | B. Russell, *Foundations of Logic 1903-05, The Collected Papers of Bertrand Russell, Vol. IV*, edited by Alasdair Urquhart with the assistance of Albert C. Lewis (London: Routledge, 1994). |

| | |
|---|---|
| *Grundlagen*: | G. Frege, *Die Grundlagen der Arithmetik: eine logisch-mathematische Untersuchung über den Begriff der Zahl*, first published 1884, Christian Thiel, ed. (Hamburg: Meiner, 1986). |
| *Grundgesetze*: | G. Frege, *Grundgesetze der Arithmetik* (Hildesheim: Olms, 1962); *The Basic Laws of Arithmetic*, trans. and ed., M. Furth (English translation of Introduction and first 52 sections) (Berkeley and Los Angeles: University of California Press, 1964). |
| *IMP*: | B. Russell, *Introduction to Mathematical Philosophy*, first published 1919, reprinted with an introduction by J. G. Slater (London: Routledge, 1993). |
| *Investigations*: | L. Wittgenstein, *Philosophical Investigations, second edition,* trans. G. E. M. Anscombe (New York: Macmillan, 1953). |
| *Lectures (1930–32)*: | D. Lee, ed., *Wittgenstein's Lectures Cambridge, 1930–32, From the notes of John King and Desmond Lee*, first published 1980, Midway Reprint (Chicago: University of Chicago Press, 1989). |
| *Lectures (1932–35)*: | A. Ambrose, ed., *Wittgenstein's Lectures Cambridge, 1932–35, From the Notes of Alice Ambrose and Margaret MacDonald*, first published 1979, Midway reprint (Chicago: University of Chicago Press, 1989). |
| *Leibniz*: | B. Russell, *The Philosophy of Leibniz*, first published 1900 (London: Routledge, 1992). |

Letters:   L. Wittgenstein, *Ludwig Wittgenstein Cambridge Letters: Correspondence with Russell, Keynes, Moore, Ramsey and Sraffa*, B. McGuinness & G. H. von Wright, eds. (Oxford: Blackwell, 1995).

LO:   L. Wittgenstein, Letters to C. K.. *Ogden with comments on the English Translation of the Tractatus Logico-Philosophicus*, G. H. von Wright, ed. (Oxford: Blackwell/RKP, 1973).

ML:   B. Russell, *Mysticism and Logic*, first published 1917 (Totowa, New Jersey: Barnes and Noble, 1981).

MPD:   B. Russell, *My Philosophical Development*, first published 1959 (London: Routledge, 1993).

Notebooks:   L. Wittgenstein, *Notebooks*, 1914–1916, edited by G. H. von Wright and G. E. M. Anscombe, trans. G. E. M. Anscombe (Oxford: Blackwell, 1961).

PE:   B. Russell, *Philosophical Essays*, first published 1910 (London: Routledge, 1994).

PG:   L. Wittgenstein, *Philosophical Grammar* (Oxford: Basil Blackwell, 1974).

POP:   B. Russell, *The Problems of Philosophy*, first published 1912 (Oxford: Oxford University Press, 1986).

PT:   L. Wittgenstein, *Prototractatus: An early version of Tractatus Logico-Philosophicus by Ludwig Wittgenstein*, B. F. McGuinness, T. Nyberg, and G. H. von Wright eds. (London: Routledge and Kegan Paul Ltd., 1971).

*Principia*:

B. Russell, *Principia Mathematica to* \*56, with A. N. Whitehead (Cambridge: Cambridge University Press, 1990).

*Principles*:

B. Russell, *The Principles of Mathematics* (London: Allen & Unwin, 1903).

*Tractatus*:

L. Wittgenstein, *Ludwig Wittgenstein Logisch-Philosophische Abhandlung: kritische Edition*, B. McGuinness and J. Schulte eds. (Frankfurt am Main: Suhrkamp, 1989). English translations: *Tractatus Logico-Philosophicus*, trans. C. K. Ogden, (London: Routledge and Kegan Paul Ltd, 1922). *Tractatus Logico-Philosophicus*, trans. D. F. Pears and B. McGuinness (London: Routledge and Kegan Paul Ltd., 1961).

# Introduction

In recent years there has been a resurgence of interest in Wittgenstein's *Tractatus Logico-Philosophicus*,[1] owed in large measure to Cora Diamond's controversial re-assessment of the aims and methods of Wittgenstein's early philosophy.[2] Diamond's revisionary reading portrays the gap between early and late Wittgenstein as far narrower than many have supposed. She regards the so-called "framing remarks" of the Preface and closing propositions as indicating that the *Tractatus* is to be read as taking seriously at every point its closing assessment of its propositions as "nonsensical."

Diamond's work has afforded us a better understanding of Wittgenstein's conception of nonsense, and—at very least—more of a sense of the *Tractatus* as an anti-metaphysical work. Whether or not one accepts Diamond's interpretation, one cannot read the *Tractatus* today without an acute awareness of the peculiar status of its contents. Certainly, nobody can now write on the *Tractatus* without giving due weight to the fact that the sentences in which the *Tractatus*' many detailed positions are framed, although seemingly[3] advertised in the Preface as expressing true *thoughts*—

---

[1] Henceforth: the "*Tractatus*."
[2] Cora Diamond, *The Realistic Spirit: Wittgenstein, Philosophy and the Mind* (Cambridge Mass.: MIT Press, 1991), ch. 6.
[3] An advocate of a Diamond-style reading might claim that the only *thoughts* communicated in the *Tractatus* are the critical statements made against other authors, together, perhaps, with the general thoughts about the nonsensical status of philosophical pronouncements.

indeed, thoughts that are "unassailable and definitive," are, by the end of the book, to be abandoned for nonsense.

It remains a matter for disagreement among scholars, however, just how Wittgenstein's famous "throwing away of the ladder" is to be interpreted. For some, the *Tractatus* is to be viewed as laying out a philosophical conception of the nature of language, logic, and the world, which "in the end" is to be recognized as precluding its own statement. On this view, the propositions of the *Tractatus* are (ultimately) to be seen as mis-fired attempts to say what can only show itself *in* language. For others, more receptive to Diamond's line, the *Tractatus* is not to be seen as conveying philosophical insights, however indirectly, but rather as undermining and destabilizing the various apparent positions set out in the *Tractatus* in the very act of formulating them.[4] On this view, we are not to look for worked out positive doctrines in the *Tractatus*, for the apparent doctrines collapse—and are intended to be seen to collapse—as we try to get clearer about them. Most importantly, even the famous "say/show" distinction is to be taken as a merely "transitional" pseudo-position that is to be exposed, at a relatively late stage in our reflections, as plain nonsense.

My goal is not to adjudicate this ongoing exegetical dispute—although much of what I say is bound to have some bearing upon it. I want, rather, to engage in a project that I see as preliminary to the resolution of these larger exegetical questions, namely a detailed investigation of the *historical* development of central aspects of Wittgenstein's early philosophy.

To be sure, the idea of such a project is scarcely new. There have been a number of more or less historical treatments of Wittgenstein's early philosophy over the years, and at least two in the last decade. [5] My feeling, however, is that the existing literature in this area leaves much work still to be done.[6]

---

[4] See, for example, Warren Goldfarb, "Metaphysics and Nonsense: on Cora Diamond's The Realistic Spirit," *Journal of Philosophical Research*, vol. 22 (1997), pp. 57-73.
[5] For example, Gordon Baker, *Wittgenstein Frege and the Vienna Circle* (Oxford: Blackwell, 1988) and Richard Brockhaus *Pulling up the Ladder: The metaphysical Roots of Wittgenstein's Tractatus Logico-Philosophicus* (La Salle, Illinois, Open Court, 1991).
[6] To my mind, neither of the works mentioned above, manages to achieve the right kind of emphasis. Baker's book, although it deals with

*Continued on next page*

The last ten years have seen the publication of several works that make an historical investigation seem particularly timely. Brian McGuinness's biography of the young Wittgenstein[7] has given us by far the deepest insight to date into the circumstances of the *Tractatus*'s composition, and his re-dating of the *Prototractatus*—placing the date of composition of its first seventy pages sometime between October 1915 and March 1916—has increased the importance of the various pre-*Tractatus* writings.[8] Moreover, with the recent publication of much of the material contained in the Russell archives, and with the appearance of Peter Hylton's illuminating historical investigation of Russell and his intellectual background,[9] we now have a much better understanding of many of the ideas to which Wittgenstein was exposed in the early stages of his career.

I plan to devote my energies to two topics that I take to be peculiarly central to Wittgenstein's early philosophy, namely Wittgenstein's views on logic and his conception of the proposition as a picture of reality. I shall approach these topics in each case by first attempting to ascertain the views to which Wittgenstein might have been responding. I shall try to bring out how Wittgenstein develops his views—or apparent views—on language and logic, as foils to the positions developed by Frege and Russell in the course of attempting to develop philosophical foundations for modern logic. I will argue that we can see the *Tractatus* as an illuminating *critical* work, whatever view we end up taking on the larger exegetical issues. (Having declared myself neutral on these issues, I should say that I do make some suggestions that bear directly on

---

the development of Wittgenstein's thought in the pre-*Tractatus* writings and with some of his responses to Frege, fails, I believe, to pay sufficient attention to the influence of Russell. Brockhaus's work, on the other hand, although it does focus on the Russellian background, fails adequately to chart the *evolution* of Wittgenstein's thinking in the years leading up to the *Tractatus*.

[7] Brian McGuinness, *Wittgenstein, a Life: Young Ludwig* (1889–1921), (London: Penguin, 1990).
[8] See Brian McGuinness, "Wittgenstein's pre-*Tractatus* manuscripts" in *Grazer Philosophische Studien* 33 (1989), pp. 35–47.
[9] Peter Hylton, *Russell, Idealism and the Emergence of Analytic Philosophy* (Oxford: Oxford University Press, 1990).

them in the concluding sections of the final chapter, but they are intended as largely conjectural.)

My governing historical thesis is that, contrary to the view of many commentators on the *Tractatus*, it is not Frege but *Russell* whose work provides the most important background for understanding what Wittgenstein is doing in the *Tractatus*. And, in particular, Russell's logical and metaphysical views, rather than his epistemology. I take this line partly because of the obvious pervasiveness of the Russellian conceptions in the *Tractatus*, but partly also because Wittgenstein's understanding of Frege seems to have been strongly distorted by his Russellian apprenticeship, and, in particular, by Russell's own highly idiosyncratic interpretation of Frege, some of which he appears to have passed on to Wittgenstein.[10]

In this connection it is important to note that several of Wittgenstein's Tractarian views—particularly those having to do with logic—were formed at a very early stage in his career, while he was studying under Russell for the B.A. at Cambridge. (Wittgenstein first introduced himself to Russell in October 1911, while attending his lectures as an unofficial auditor. In February 1912 he became a member of Trinity college, but his academic relationship with Russell, although by then firmly established, was not formalized until June 1912, with the appointment of Russell as his supervisor. Wittgenstein continued to discuss issues in the philosophy of logic and mathematics with Russell, either in person or through correspondence, until the end of 1913 when Wittgenstein's departure for Norway and his subsequent military service brought philosophical dialogue to a close. Conversation did not resume until 1919, when Wittgenstein wrote to Russell to inform him of the existence of the *Tractatus*.[11])

The influence of Russell is particularly evident in the *Notes on Logic* of October 1913,[12] which Wittgenstein regarded as a summary of the work he had done in his two years at Cambridge.[13] Importantly, some of the views in these notes appear to have ger-

---

[10]  See chapter II for further details.
[11]  For further details see McGuinness *Wittgenstein* chs. 4 & 5.
[12]  *Notebooks*, Appendix 1, pp. 93–107.
[13]  In his letter of 20th September 1913, Wittgenstein wrote to Russell requesting a meeting in which he would "give [Russell] a survey of the whole field of what [he had] done up to now" (*Letters*, p. 39). This was duly arranged, and the notes Wittgenstein dictated to Russell the following month became the "Summary" section of the *Notes on Logic*.

minated at a time when Wittgenstein saw himself as developing positions *in conjunction with* Russell. We find Wittgenstein writing to Russell in the summer of 1912 that "*our* problems can be traced down to atomic propositions" (my emphasis)[14] and in December of the same year that "...I had a long discussion with Frege about *our* theory of symbolism"[15] (my emphasis again). Because Wittgenstein drew heavily on the *Notes on Logic* in composing the *Tractatus*—he copied many of the remarks from the *Notes* straight into the *Tractatus*—the influence of Russell during this period takes on a particular importance.

In 1913 the letters assume a less collaborative tone. Now Wittgenstein talks about "his" problems[16] and he becomes openly critical of Russell's views. He faults Russell's "multiple relation theory of judgement" for failing to make it impossible to judge nonsense; he criticizes Russell's axioms of reducibility and infinity for being non-logical, and he deems the Theory of Types "superfluous."[17] Nonetheless, it is clear that Wittgenstein continued to see some overlap between his *problems* and Russell's. In a letter of March 1919, written from a prison camp in Cassino,[18] Wittgenstein tells Russell: "I believe I've solved our problems finally." Evidently, however, the solution is achieved only by rejecting the fruits of the earlier collaboration. Wittgenstein continues: "[The *Tractatus*] upsets all our theory of truth, of classes, of numbers and all the rest."

During the period of their collaboration the project on which Russell and Wittgenstein were engaged was one of developing metaphysical underpinnings for the logic of *Principia*. This foundation had not been adequately provided when *Principia* went to press. (For example, the *Principia*'s account of the bearer of truth and falsehood, namely, the multiple relation theory of judgement—is disengaged from the system of *Principia*, which operates with an ontology of propositions.) It is not clear how far their col-

---

[14] Letter to Russell, Summer 1912, *Letters*, p. 20.
[15] In the letter of 16th August 1912 Wittgenstein speaks of "our troubles" being "overcome by assuming different sorts of relations of signs to things," and again of "our problem" (*Letters*, p. 19).
[16] The letter of 22nd July 1913 contains the following remarks "My problems get clearer now"; "I have not solved one of my problems..." (*Letters*, p. 33)
[17] Each of these points is made in one or other letter of 1913.
[18] *Letters*, p. 111.

laborative efforts got, but it does seem likely that Wittgenstein thought of himself as continuing this project independently of Russell for several years to come.[19]

In addition to these historical circumstances, there are a number of textual factors that point to Russell as the most important influence on Wittgenstein. For one thing, Russellian terminology predominates in the *Tractatus*. Wittgenstein speaks of: "complexes," "the verb of the proposition," "internal and external relations," "logical sum," "logical product," and "the assertion sign." [20] Each of these expressions is Russellian in origin and is not found in Frege's writings. Of course, Fregean terminology is also present in the *Tractatus*, but, unlike the Russellian terminology, it tends to be used with a sense its originator did not intend. The Fregean term "logical object," for example, is used by Wittgenstein to refer to Frege's and Russell's logical constants (hence to functions), not—or not *only*[21]—to Fregean value-ranges.[22] And the term "thought," which for Frege connotes something non-linguistic, signifies something linguistic for Wittgenstein.[23]

Nor is Wittgenstein very careful about distinguishing Frege's positions from Russell's. Very often in the *Tractatus* Russell and Frege are mentioned in the same breath, almost as if they had co-authored a single logical treatise. At one point Wittgenstein even refers to "The logical symbolism of Frege and Russell" as if to imply that the differences between their symbolisms can be ignored for philosophical purposes (3.325). This blurring of the distinction between Frege and Russell is exacerbated by Wittgenstein's tendency to read into Frege's work conceptions that are quite alien to Frege's thinking. One key example, which I discuss at some length in chapter II, is the Russellian notion of the "verb of the proposition."

---

[19] A broadening occurs in August 1916, when Wittgenstein announces: "Yes, my work has broadened out from the foundations of logic to the essence of the world" (*Notebooks*, p. 79) (translation my own).

[20] Frege uses only the expression "the judgement stroke."

[21] See 4.441, where Wittgenstein makes it clear that if—*per impossibile*—truth-functions were objects, they would count as logical objects.

[22] See, for example, *Grundgesetze* II, § 74.

[23] "Thoughts," for Wittgenstein, are "significant proposition[s]" (4). But since propositions are propositional *signs* in their projective relation to the world, this makes them linguistic in character.

In exploring the development of Wittgenstein's ideas I have made quite heavy use of Wittgenstein's pre-*Tractatus* writings, particularly the 1913 *Notes on Logic* and the 1914 *Notes Dictated to G. E. Moore in Norway*. I should say a word in justification of this practice. I take these texts to have a particular authority among the pre-*Tractatus* writings, for there is evidence that Wittgenstein regarded them—in contrast to the *Notebooks*—as having the status of finished works; works, moreover, whose content he still *believed* at the time of beginning to write the manuscript which became known as the *Prototractatus*. In a letter of July 22nd, 1915 Wittgenstein tells Russell that he regards the *Moore Notes* "essentially as definitive"[24] and that in the event of his death Russell is to get "his manuscript printed whether anyone understands it or not." (This manuscript is most likely the one Wittgenstein sent to Russell from Norway in October 1913;[25] it contains what became the four "manuscript" sections [26] of the *Notes on Logic*.[27])

If McGuinness is correct,[28] this letter would have been written only a few months before Wittgenstein began composing a "summary" of his earlier ideas[29]—a document that McGuinness estimates he wrote between October 1915 and March 1916, and which we know as the first seventy sides of *Prototractatus*. So there is good reason to think that these documents contain material that closely reflects views Wittgenstein held while beginning to write the *Prototractatus*, a work which itself corresponds quite closely to the *Tractatus*. Moreover, it is clear that Wittgenstein regarded the *Tractatus* as drawing on some of the ideas in the 1913 *Notes*. In the letter of March 1919 he remarks: "I've written a book called "Logisch-Philosophische Abhandlung" containing all my work of the last *six* years" (my emphasis). The wartime *Notebooks* do not have anything like the authority of these two earlier works, but because they contain much information relating

---

[24] *Letters*, p. 102.
[25] The manuscript is mentioned in the postscript to the letter of 29th October 1913, *Letters*, pp. 45–6.
[26] The manuscripts were translated into English by Russell.
[27] See the letter to Russell of the 22nd May 1915, *Letters*, p. 102. It is not altogether clear whether Wittgenstein means the *Moore Notes* or the *Notes on Logic* here, but since he has already referred the to former as "Moore's notes" in this letter, it seems most likely that "his manuscript" refers to the manuscript sections of the *Notes on Logic*.
[28] McGuinness, op. cit., pp. 35—47.
[29] Ibid.

to the development of Wittgenstein's views, I have made some—more cautious—use of them too.

The book divides into four largely self-contained studies, which are unified by a common interpretive approach. I open with a discussion of Wittgenstein's conception of logic as tautologous, focusing on central exegetical questions that have been relatively neglected in the secondary literature. In the second chapter, I turn to an examination of Wittgenstein's attack on the notion of "logical assertion." I argue that, at its deepest level, this attack amounts to a successful critique of a conception of the proposition espoused both by the early Russell and by the Frege of *Begriffsschrift*. In the third chapter I explore Wittgenstein's so-called "picture theory" of the proposition. I argue first that it furnishes an account of the relationship between language and the proposition that is missing from Russell's *Principles*, and secondly that it provides for a dissolution of the problem of the unity of the proposition. In the final chapter I explore Wittgenstein's critique of Frege's and Russell's "laws of inference." I argue that Wittgenstein is primarily concerned with opposing a Russellian conception of the nature of logical entailment, a view which portrays entailment as an external relation somehow "grounded" in the laws of logic. I present Wittgenstein's positive views as a natural response to Russell's anti-Bradlean doctrine that all relations—including logical relations—are "external." The chapter is intended to illustrate an approach to reading the apparently positive doctrines of the *Tractatus* that is compatible with their having an unofficial or "transitional" status.

Finally, a note on the translation of passages from the *Tractatus*. My general practice has been to follow whichever of the two established translations of Wittgenstein's *Logisch-Philosophische Abhandlung* seems most accurate in the case at hand. Where neither translation seems suitable I have added my own, with a note to that effect. I have followed the standard practice of referring to passages from the *Tractatus* by citing the decimal number of the "proposition" to which they belong.

LOGIC AND LANGUAGE IN WITTGENSTEIN'S
*TRACTATUS*

# CHAPTER I

# Logic

## INTRODUCTION

In the *Tractatus* Wittgenstein dismisses a view of logic he finds in the works of Frege and Russell:

> Theories that make a proposition of logic appear to have content are always false. (6.*111*)

> The correct explanation of logical propositions must give them a peculiar position among all propositions. (6.*112*)

> The mark of a logical proposition is *not* general validity. (6.*1231*)

> Logic is not a theory but a reflection of the world. (6.*13*)

The view being rejected here has been dubbed the "universalist conception of logic."[30] On this view, logic is a theory of the most general features of reality. Its axioms are fully contentful, non-schematic, general propositions. They differ from non-logical truths, not in kind, but only in their degree of generality. They are

---

[30] For further discussion of the universalist conception see Jean van Heijenoort, "Logic as Calculus and Logic as Language," *Synthese* 17 (1967), pp. 324–30. Warren Goldfarb, "Logic in the Twenties: the Nature of the Quantifier," *Journal of Symbolic Logic* 44 (1979), pp. 351–68, and Thomas Ricketts, "Objectivity and Objecthood: Frege's Metaphysics of Judgement," in *Frege Synthesized*, Leila Haaparanta and Jaakko Hintikka eds. (Boston: D. Reidel Publishing Co., 1986), pp. 65–95.

"fully generalized" in that they contain no topic-specific vocabu-lary.[31] Wittgenstein rejects this conception for two reasons.

First, the view conflicts with Wittgenstein's commitment to the "bi-polarity" of the proposition. In the 1913 *Notes on Logic* the bi-polarity of genuine propositions is characterized in terms of their being "essentially true-false" (*Notebooks*, p. 98). By their very nature they are capable both of truth and of falsity.[32] The bi-polarity of a proposition is disclosed through our capacity to understand both what would be the case for it to be true and what would be the case for it to be false. If I cannot form a full concep-tion of both situations, I do not understand the proposition. (*Notebooks*, pp. 94–5 and 98–9.)[33]

The laws of logic, as Frege and Russell construe them, fail to meet the requirement of bi-polarity.[34] As the conditions of coherent conceiving, these laws are supposed to hold in every conceivable world, but that precludes our being able to say how the world would look if any of them failed to hold. Since they maintain that the propositions of logic are nonetheless genuine, contentful propositions, Frege and Russell implicitly reject the requirement of bi-polarity.

In the *Tractatus* Wittgenstein raises an objection that is less dependent on his own commitments. He claims that the Frege-Russell conception of logic fails to do justice to our sense that the propositions of logic have a *unique* status among propositions. He puts the point by saying that for Frege and Russell the laws of logic take on the character of propositions of natural science (6.*111*).

---

[31] There is a well-known problem with taking this characterization as a *specification* of the propositions of logic. It is simply not clear what is to count as "topic-universal vocabulary." Frege does not address this ques-tion, and Russell, despairing of giving any non-circular characterization, contents himself with the answer that the logical constants are to be defined by enumeration (*Principles*, § 10)

[32] Although bi-polarity is not explicitly mentioned in the *Tractatus*, Wittgenstein is unlikely to have changed his mind about it. He mentions the requirement as late as the *Notebooks* entry for the 2nd of June, 1915 (*Notebooks*, p. 53). If McGuinness is right, this would have been only a few months before he set about writing the first seventy sides of the *Prototractatus*.

[33] *Letters*, p. 47.

[34] See Russell's 1902 paper "The Study of Mathematics," in *Mysticism and Logic*, first published 1917, reprinted by Barnes and Noble 1981. Frege, *Die Grundlagen der Arithmetik*, eine *logisch-mathematische Untersuchung über den Begriff der Zahl* (Breslau, 1884), § 14.

He means that they are accorded the status of (especially compendious) generalizations, which report on the world as it actually stands. To Wittgenstein this fails to do justice to our sense that they occupy a privileged place in our conceptual scheme; it fails to register that the propositions of logic are fundamentally different in kind from those of natural science (6.111 & 6.112).[35, 36]

For Wittgenstein, the solution to these problems is to jettison the idea that logic has content. Logic is to be viewed not as a set of general laws, but as a body of sentences, which, because they convey no information (4.461), are to be regarded as expressing no thoughts. In the *Tractatus* these sentences—which we should today call "logical truths"— are labelled "tautologies" (6.1) in order to draw attention to their emptiness.[37] They "say nothing" (6.11), have no sense, are *sinnlos* (4.461); and, lacking sense, they make no claims on the world. They "stand in no presenting relation to reality" and so are not "pictures of reality" (4.462). But because, for Wittgenstein, sentences can be true or false *only* by picturing reality (4.06), this means that tautologies cannot be truths—at least not in the strict sense of the word.[38]

---

[35] This second point is a direct descendant of one of Wittgenstein's earliest epiphanies. In a letter to Russell of June 22, 1912 he pronounces, with disarming confidence, that, contrary to what Russell had supposed, "Logic must turn out to be of a TOTALLY different kind than any other science" (*Letters*, p. 15).

[36] There are also hints at 6.111 of an *ad hominem* argument against Russell. Suppose, as Wittgenstein supposes, that Frege and Russell required the propositions of logic to be self-evident (5.4731 & 6.1271). Additionally assume, as Russell at one stage assumed, that the law of excluded middle can be understood as saying that every proposition has exactly one of two simple, indefinable properties: truth and falsehood. With these assumptions in place, the self-evidence of the law of excluded middle simply vanishes. It now sounds no more self-evident than the claim that all roses are red or yellow would sound if it were true. This argument only has force against Russell if he did indeed take self-evidence to be essential to logic. Because I find that doubtful, I would not rest much weight on it.

[37] Dreben and Floyd argue persuasively that Wittgenstein chose to call the propositions of logic "tautologies" precisely because of the connotations of emptiness, triflingness etc., that the term carries in the writings of Russell and others. (Burton Dreben & Juliet Floyd, "Tautology: How not to use a word," *Synthese* 87 (1991), pp. 23–49.)

[38] Given Wittgenstein's view that the characteristic mark of logical propositions is that "one can recognize from the symbol alone that they are true" (6.113), one might wonder whether he wasn't simply inconsistent on the question whether tautologies are true. For a view of this kind see Robert Fogelin, *Wittgenstein*, second edition (London: Routledge &

*Continued on next page*

In this chapter I want to work towards a deeper understanding of this view of logic by probing some of its more puzzling features. I shall focus on three questions that have been relatively neglected in the existing literature. First, if tautologies and contradictions have no sense, why are they nonetheless "continuous" with senseful propositions,[39] and to be regarded as "part of the symbolism" (4.4611)? Why are they not nonsense (cf. 4.4611)? Secondly, how are we to understand Wittgenstein's view that negation, conjunction and disjunction are "operations" (5.2341); and what might have led him to such a view? Thirdly, in what sense could it be correct to say that there can never be "surprises" in logic (6.1251)? These questions provide the framework for this chapter, though others will be engaged *en route*.

## [1] LOGIC AS SINNLOS

At 4.4611, having made the celebrated observation that tautology and contradiction are without sense (*sinnlos*), Wittgenstein enters an equally famous qualification:

> Tautology and contradiction are, however, not nonsensical (*unsinnig*); they are part of the symbolism, in the same way that "0" is part of the symbolism of arithmetic.

---

& Kegan Paul Ltd., 1987), pp. 45–7. However, there is plenty of evidence to support the idea that when Wittgenstein calls a tautology "true," he intends this only in an honorary sense. For example, at 6.125, when speaking of true logical propositions Wittgenstein takes care to enclose the word "true" in shudder quotes. And in the 1914 *Moore Notes* he speaks of "what is called the truth of a logical proposition" (*Notebooks*, p. 108), remarking a page later that "logical propositions are neither true nor false" (*Notebooks*, p. 109). Moreover, there is a further argument that tautologies are not to be regarded as true. If tautologies were true in every possible situation, Wittgenstein would have to regard them as confirmed by every possible experience. But this is something that he expressly denies:

> This [account of the propositions of logic] throws light on the question why logical propositions can no more be empirically confirmed than they can be empirically refuted. Not only must a proposition of logic be incapable of being contradicted by any possible experience, but it must also be incapable of being confirmed by any such. (6.1222)

[39] *Lectures*, (1932–35), p. 137.

That they are not nonsense, and are in some sense part of the symbolism, seems undeniable. They cannot be nonsense because they may (in some sense) occur as "parts" of meaningful propositions. For example, "(pv¬p).q" is a propositional sign with sense; it says the same thing as "q" (cf. 4.465). But this would not be so if the tautology out of which it is constructed were a mere string of nonsense. Tautologies are part of the symbolism because any language containing all the logical operators must generate them. If "It is raining" is a meaningful sentence, and if the operations of negation and disjunction apply to all meaningful sentences, then "Either it is raining or it is not raining" must be meaningful (i.e. non-nonsensical) too.

But what is it about tautologies (and contradictions) that enables them to lack sense without being nonsense? The beginnings of an answer are provided by Cora Diamond's important observation that for the early Wittgenstein a nonsensical sentence is to be thought of as resulting not from the inappropriate combination of meaningful words, but from the presence in a sentence of words that lack a meaning (cf. 5.4733).[40] If Diamond is right, we might expect (part of) Wittgenstein's explanation of why a tautology is not nonsense to run along similar lines.[41] And, indeed, in the one place where Wittgenstein discusses the question, this is just what we find. In the 1914 *Notes Dictated to G.E. Moore in Norway*[42] he writes:

> A tautology (*not* a logical proposition) is not nonsense in the same sense in which, e.g., a proposition in which words which have no meaning occur is nonsense. What happens in it is that all its simple parts have meaning, but it is such that the connections between these paralyse or destroy one anoth-

---

[40] See, for example, Diamond, *The Realistic Spirit*, ch. 3.
[41] To prevent this characterization from making it trivially the case that there are no nonsensical sentences, one would need to supplement it with an account of the notion of a "word" that does not build it in that words have meanings. (So, for example, one could not characterize a word as a *meaningful* unit of language that is semantically simple in the sense that none of its parts make a systematic contribution to its meaning.) Presumably, one would need to draw on the resources of syntactic theory, and argue that some crisply characterized notion of a minimal sentential constituent either cashes, or is at least analogous to, what Wittgenstein tacitly had in mind by the notion of a simple sign. The prospects for such an account are uncertain, but also—mercifully—beyond the scope of this inquiry.
[42] *Notebooks*, Appendix 2, pp. 108–119.

er, so that they are all connected only in some irrelevant manner. (*Notebooks,* p. 118)

Wittgenstein enters the qualification "*simple* parts" because, in the broad sense of "meaning" that is in play here—namely, one according to which a sign has "meaning" just in case it makes a non-null contribution to the meaning of the wholes in which it occurs, [43] certain *complex* components of tautologies may indeed lack a "meaning" without rendering the whole *unsinnig*. For example, because the operation of disjoining a tautology is the identity operation on propositions, a tautology such as "p.¬pv¬(p.¬p)" may be regarded as containing complex disjuncts that make only a null contribution to the sense of the whole; however, because each of this tautology's *simple* parts makes a non-null contribution, the whole is not *unsinnig*.

By the *Tractatus* the early metaphors of a "paralysis" or "destruction" of connections have partially crystallized into the (slightly) clearer notion of a *cancellation* of (what amount to) truth-conditions.[44, 45] "In the tautology," says Wittgenstein, "the conditions of agreement with the world—the presenting relations—cancel one another,[46] so that it stands in no presenting relation to reality" (4.462). The truth-conditions may be thought to "cancel one another" because they are the truth-conditions of propositions whose senses are, metaphorically speaking, "equal and opposite":

---

[43]   This broad sense of "meaning" is also in play in the *Notebooks's* remark of six months later: "Roughly speaking, before any proposition can make sense at all the logical constants must have meaning (*Bedeutung*)" (*Notebooks,* p. 15). Seeing that already, by the 1913 *Notes on Logic,* Wittgenstein has arrived at the view that the logical constants signify by expressing so-called "ab-operations," rather than by having references (*Notebooks,* p. 94), it would be oddly retrograde—*pace* Anscombe's editorial note—for him to mean "reference" here.

[44]   Cf. the *Notebooks* entry for 2nd November 1914 (*Notebooks,* p. 24).

[45]   The less helpful notion of the *destruction* of connections also survives in the rather obscure remarks at 4.466 & 4.4661.

[46]   Wittgenstein uses "*aufheben*" here. I have heard it suggested that he may be playing with the Hegelian resonances of this word. However, "*aufheben*" has a usage, going back (at least) to Kant, on which it simply means "to cancel out." Kant uses it this way in the *Critique* when speaking of the cancelling out of opposed natural forces (See A265/B320 & A273/B329).

Tautology and contradiction are without sense (*sinnlos*).
(Like the point from which two arrows go out in opposite
directions.) (4.461)

As Erik Stenius long ago observed, Wittgenstein is here pun-
ning on "*Sinn*," which can mean both "sense" and "direction."[47]
The two arrows of 4.461 are analogous to the two equal but opposite senses of the propositions "p" and "¬p," which in a tautology
or contradiction are so combined as to yield a senseless (hence
directionless) whole. In a logical proposition the senses of the component propositions are said to be *in equilibrium*:

> In a logical proposition propositions are brought into equi-
> librium [*ins Gleichgewicht gebracht*] with one another, and
> the state of equilibrium [*der Zustand des Gleichgewichts*]
> then shows how these propositions must be logically con-
> structed. (6.121)

The word "*Gleichgewicht*"—literally "equal weight"—suggests the idea of a balance of *forces*. A similar idea is suggested by
Wittgenstein's explanation to Ogden of what he had intended at
6.121 in calling "the method of combining propositions into
propositions which say nothing" a "null-method" (*Nullmethode*):

> "Nullmethode" in German is an expression used in physics;
> when—for instance—you measure an electric resistance by
> regulating another resistance until the galvanometer points to
> 0 again we call this a "Nullmethode." [48]

The suggestion of 6.121 thus seems to be that in constructing
logical propositions we bring about a state of equilibrium in something *roughly* analogous to the manner in which we bring about an
equilibrium of electrical fields within a circuit.

---

[47]   Erik Stenius, *Wittgenstein's "Tractatus": A critical exposition of its
main lines of thought* (Ithaca, New York: Cornell University Press, 1960).
In the *Tractatus* the use of "*Sinn*" to mean direction is clearest at 3.144,
where Wittgenstein remarks: "Names are like points; propositions like
arrows—they have sense." "*Sinn*" appears with the meaning of "direction" most commonly in compound nouns. In "*Drehsinn*" and
"*Uhrzeigersinn*," for example, it refers to a direction of rotation—in the
latter case, of the hands of a clock. (I am grateful to Dirk Lumma and
Markus Stepanians for these linguistic points.)
[48]   *LO*, p. 34.

The electrical metaphor is also suggestive in another way. When an electrical circuit is in a state of equilibrium everything in it is functioning normally: everything is in place for current to flow, for *work* to be done; however, owing to the details of the circuit's construction, the opposed potentials cancel one another out so that no current flows. Likewise, in a tautology everything in what we might imagine as the "linguistic circuit" is in place and functioning normally; no simple sign is lacking a meaning. However, owing to the particular way in which it is put together, a tautology combines the senses of several propositions in such a way that they cancel one another out. So even though a tautology is properly constructed, it can convey no information, do no *linguistic* work.

It is important to recognize that in a tautology even the logical constants have a "meaning" in the broad sense. For although they do not signify by having reference,[49] they do have meaning in the sense of making a non-null contribution to the sense—or in the case of tautology and contradiction the *sinnlosigkeit*—of sentences in which they figure. Their contribution is to indicate the manner in which certain propositions are combined, or otherwise operated upon.[50] The caveat "or otherwise operated upon" is required because the negation sign can hardly be thought to signify a mode of *combination*. Negation, rather, is conceived as an operation that reverses a proposition's sense (5.2341). Judging by a later reflection, Wittgenstein appears to have been thinking of a proposition and its negation by analogy with oppositely signed magnitudes, which, when conjoined or disjoined, as it were, "sum" to yield a zero *quantity* of sense: [51]

---

[49]  This is the lesson of the *Tractatus's* famous *Grundgedanke*: "My fundamental thought is that the 'logical constants' do not represent [*nicht vertreten*]" (4.0312).

[50]  This claim can seem to be in tension with Wittgenstein's remark at 5.25 that "the occurrence of an operation does not characterize the sense of a proposition" (5.25). However, given that Wittgenstein's point there is to distinguish operations from functions, it seems most likely that he intends to be contrasting his view with Russell's view according to which "¬¬p" and "p" are taken to express different propositions simply because the former contains propositional elements that the latter lacks. Wittgenstein's point is that the presence of the sign for an operation in a propositional sign is not by itself sufficient to affect the sense of the proposition. This is not, however, to deny that "p" and "¬p" have different senses in virtue of the occurrence in one but not the other of the sign for the operation of negation.

[51]  Although it would be dangerous to put too much weight on this figu-

*Continued on next page*

When I called tautologies "senseless" I meant to stress a connection with a quantity of sense, namely 0. (*Lectures* (*1932–35*), pp. 136–7)

Our discussion of operations suggests a further reason why tautology and contradiction ought to be considered continuous with other signs: they are constructed—ultimately from elementary propositions—by means of the very same logical operations that are employed in the construction of senseful propositions. Their distinctness lies *solely* in the fact that, in their case, the logical operators effect a cancellation of senses.

This explanation is satisfying up to a point, but it also invites further questions. How exactly are we to think of the "operations" in question? And what are they to be thought of as operations upon? Because tautologies and contradictions can occur as *sinnlos* constituents of senseful propositions, we cannot, in general, treat *senses* as the relevant operanda. Instead, we shall need to think of the "truth-operations" as operating in the first instance on something that may or may not have a sense. If we could understand what *this* item is supposed to be, the way would be clear to thinking of operations on senses as performed by means of operations on a special class of more basic items. The idea would be akin to the one involved in the suggestion that we might think of operations upon abstract objects—for example, the operation of writing down Gödel's theorem—as brought about by means of related operations on certain concrete entities appropriately related to them—for example, the operation of writing down a token of a sentence expressing Gödel's theorem.[52] (However, there is only a loose kinship between the two ideas. Aside from anything else, Wittgenstein would never have regarded senses as abstract objects.[53])

---

rative comparison, we might think of conjunction and disjunction as corresponding to the two ways of arranging line vectors so that they add to zero, viz. "->&lt;-" and "&lt;—>." (This idea comes under strain as soon as we consider propositions containing more than one occurrence of a given sentence.)

[52] The idea is originally due to Helen Cartwright. It is discussed in the introduction to Richard Cartwright's *Philosophical Essays* (Cambridge, Mass.: MIT Press, 1987).

[53] Compare *Notebooks*, p. 102: "Neither the sense nor the meaning of a proposition is a thing."

## [2] LOGICAL OPERATIONS AND THEIR OPERANDA

It will help to begin our investigation with a discussion of the "ab-notation" of the 1913 *Notes on Logic*. Consider the following three propositions written in the ab-notation.

(1)  a-p-b
(2)  b-a-p-b-a
(3)  a-b-a-p-b-a-b

If (1) says that p, then (2) says that not-p; and (3), in turn, is (2)'s negation, and so once again says that p. What says that p in (1) and (3) is the "symbolizing fact" *in* each of these items. In the *Notes on Logic* Wittgenstein explains this idea in the following way:

> The symbolising fact in a-p-b is that, SAY a is on the left of p and b on the right of p. (*Notebooks*, p. 94)

We might describe the symbolizing fact common to (1) and (3) as the fact that 'a' and 'b' occur *in that order* as the *outer* poles of some appropriately constructed string of signs.[54] (The notion of an "appropriately constructed string of signs" will be explicable in terms of certain rules for forming more complex signs out of simpler ones. An appropriate string will be one that has been generated from specified elements by a finite number of applications of some specified set of purely syntactic operations.)

Both of the strings written down after "(1)" and "(3)" can be said to "token"[55] this fact, for they can each be regarded as making true the statement that "a" and "b" occur *in that order* as the *outer* poles of some appropriately constructed string of signs (a different string in each case).

---

[54] The idea of identifying symbolizing facts in this way is suggested by Wittgenstein's remark in the 1914 *Moore Notes* that (1) and (3), as well as having the same meaning, are the same *symbol* (*Notebooks*, pp. 114–15). "a" and "b" are best thought of as syntactic items which have no significance of their own, but which figure in the subject-matter of a "symbolizing fact," which does have significance. I would conjecture that Wittgenstein uses these signs, rather than "T" and "F," to stress that they have no meaning of their own, but are given significance only by giving significance to the whole fact in whose subject-matter they figure.

[55] Here I am making do. I know of no altogether satisfactory word for the relation between an object and a fact about it.

For expository purposes it will be convenient to have a term for the item that tokens a symbolizing fact. Let us call it an "Inscription."[56] (Although Inscriptions "token" symbolizing facts, they should themselves be thought of as types, capable of having multiple tokenings.) As Wittgenstein makes clear, some facts about the Inscription are irrelevant to the symbolizing fact it tokens. For example, the Inscription's orientation and arrangement on the page is not of any consequence.[57] The symbolizing fact, however, is essential to the proposition: it cannot be altered without altering the proposition's sense.[58]

I want to propose that we think of operations on propositions [59] as achieved by means of operations on symbolizing facts, and that these latter operations should, in turn, be understood as achieved by means of syntactic operations upon Inscriptions. When we operate on one symbolizing fact and obtain another as the result of the operation, we bring it about that the Inscription tokening the symbolizing fact to be operated upon now occurs as a part of the Inscription tokening the result of the operation. So, for example, when we negate proposition (1) we do so by bringing it about that the symbolizing fact in (2) obtains, and this is something we achieve by constructing the Inscription in (2) from the Inscription in (1). The rule governing the construction might be stated: "add a new set of outer poles according to the following rule: draw an 'a' if the old pole was 'b', and *vice versa*." This syntactic operation has the effect of reversing the polarity of the proposition. If the proposition has a sense, it reverses that sense by reversing the order of the poles; if, on the other hand, the proposition is a tautology or a contradiction, the rule generates a *unipolar* propositional sign

---

[56] Wittgenstein treats names as classes of tokens (*Notebooks*, p. 102). In a similar spirit we might identify Inscriptions with classes of similar Inscription-tokens.

[57] Cf. the letter to Russell of 1913 (*Letters*, p. 47).

[58] Cf. 4.465: "The essence of the symbol cannot be altered without altering its sense." I am reading "symbol" here as meaning "symbolizing fact."

[59] I am following Wittgenstein in using "proposition" as a term for any symbolizing fact that results from the iterated application of truth-operations to elementary propositions. According to this usage, some propositions will have senses and some, being tautologies or contradictions, will lack them. It is because Wittgenstein allows for *sinnlos* propositions that he characterizes the thought at 4 as the "significant (*sinnvolle*) proposition." He is not, however, consistent in this usage. See, for example, 4.464.

of the opposite polarity—where a "unipolar" propositional sign is one all of whose *genuine* outer poles are the same. (The qualification is needed because when the sign is constructed from more than one instance of the same proposition not all of the "outer poles" will be traceable back to genuine "truth-combinations," i.e., to *consistent* combinations of inner poles. For an illustration of how non-genuine poles are generated see the *Moore Notes* (*Notebooks*, p. 115).)

Insofar as the operation involves the construction of one Inscription out of another, it may be thought of as effecting the construction of one *symbolizing fact* out of another. However, one symbolizing fact cannot, strictly speaking, be regarded as a *part* of another: a fact about a part of an Inscription is not a part of a fact about the whole. The component symbolizing fact should rather be thought of as constituting an, in some cases inessential,[60] *stage* in the construction of a more complex sign. In the *Tractatus* Wittgenstein speaks of the "propositional sign" rather than the "symbolizing fact." But, since the propositional sign is a *fact* (*3.14*), it is plausible to suppose that the *Tractatus*'s "propositional sign" is just the descendant of the "symbolizing fact" of the *Notes on Logic*.

In general, propositions may be combined by standing as bases to the operations corresponding to any non-unary connectives.[61] But because the set of connectives {¬, &} is truth-functionally adequate, and because for Wittgenstein quantification is to be analysed in terms of truth-functional operations, we need only consider the case of conjunction. In the *Tractatus*' TF-notation, we

---

[60] Logically complex propositions represent *inessential* steps in the construction of other more complex propositions because each proposition can be thought of as constructed directly from elementary propositions by means of a single operation (of the appropriate complexity) upon elementary propositions (5.3).

[61] Wittgenstein himself envisaged using a generalization of the Sheffer stroke—the N-ope*r*ator—for the combination of propositions. This is best viewed as a, so to speak, "n-ary operator" for arbitrary (and possibly infinite) n. However, for purposes of grasping the idea of a truth-operator it is more helpful to focus on binary connectives, as, indeed, did Wittgenstein himself (See *6.1203*).

conjoin p and q by operating upon them in such a way as to create a propositional sign whose Inscription looks like this:

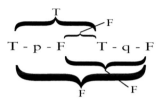

In this notation constituent propositions are combined in the very manner displayed by the Inscription that provides the subject-matter for the symbolizing fact. In this case they are connected in such a way that any combination of poles other than {T,T} yields F. What combines the component propositions is the rule for determining the polarity of the whole from the polarities of its parts. In the case of a tautology the relevant rules generate a unipolar propositional sign out of signs that may or may not be unipolar. Because the *same* rules apply both to uni- and bi-polar propositional signs, there need be no mystery about how the truth-operations can operate on *sinnlos* propositions.

## [3] LOGICAL CONNECTIVES AS PUNCTUATION

At 5.4611 Wittgenstein says: "Signs for logical operations are punctuation marks." It is clear that he means to suggest an analogy between these two classes of signs, founded upon the manner in which they signify. Peter Hylton has recently suggested one form the analogy might take.[62] According to Hylton, the logical connectives resemble punctuation marks in that both kinds of sign are essential to the meanings of the sentences in which they occur, even though they lack a meaning of their own. Hylton's suggestion points in the right direction, but is not strictly correct. It is true that for Wittgenstein the logical connectives lack sense and (Fregean) reference, but false that they lack a meaning of their own in the sense in which Hylton's example of a "punctuation mark" lacks a meaning of its own. Hylton focuses on the example of parentheses used to indicate the scope of the logical connectives.

---

[62] Peter Hylton, "Functions, Operations and Sense in Wittgenstein's *Tractatus*," in W. Tait ed., *Early Analytic Philosophy* (Chicago, Illinois: Open Court, 1997), pp. 91–105.

As Hylton notes, Wittgenstein himself regards these signs as having no meaning in their own right (5.461). However, for Wittgenstein, that is because, on the view he is considering, parentheses function as semantically insignificant parts of other signs that are regarded as semantically simple. On such a view, the parentheses in "p⊃(q⊃r)," for example, are regarded as indicating one argument place of the relational expression "( )⊃( )," the other pair of parentheses being considered "present but not written in" for the usual reasons of perspicuity and typographical convenience.

If *this* were the sense in which the logical connectives had "no meaning of their own," we would have to say that the presence of the sign "and" in the two sentences: "It is raining and it is windy" and "John wept and Jean whooped" no more signifies something common to their meanings than does the presence of the string of letters "cat" in the words "cattle" and "catatonic." And that is plainly false. Despite lacking their own sense or reference, the logical connectives do have a meaning of their own insofar as they make a *uniform* contribution to the meanings of the sentences in which they occur.

A symptom of the trouble with Hylton's suggestion is that it forces a poor choice of example. Scope-indicating devices after all compare unfavourably, as paradigms of *punctuation*, with the comma and the full-stop. The latter are signs that, although they lack sense and reference, nonetheless do have a meaning in their own right in the sense Hylton is concerned with. Consider, for example, the following two sentences, which differ from each other only with respect to a comma.

4) The chef watched her assistant, stirring the soup.
5) The chef watched her assistant stirring the soup.

To my ear—or eye—(4) means that the chef watched her assistant while she (the chef) was stirring the soup, while (5) means that the chef watched her assistant perform the act of stirring the soup. In this example, the whole of the difference between the meanings of the two sentences is the difference indicated by the comma, for the meanings of the other constituents are the same in both sentences. But the comma, plainly, is far from being a semantically inert part of another sign.

Wittgenstein's point is that the logical connectives share with punctuation marks the feature of lacking sense and reference while nonetheless having a meaning in their own right. The point of the comparison with punctuation is to bring out that the logical connectives make a *purely structural* contribution to the meanings of the sentences in which they figure.

## [4] PERSPICUOUS NOTATION

In addition to reinterpreting Russell's notation, Wittgenstein presents a number of alternatives to it. There is the TF-notation, which we have briefly examined, but also the truth-table and N-operator notations (See 4.442 & 5.5 ff.). The proliferation of alternatives suggests that Wittgenstein is trying to find a notation that embodies as much as possible of the philosophical picture of language and logic set forth in the *Tractatus*. No one of Wittgenstein's notations embodies every aspect of this conception, but each, in its own way, succeeds in bringing out one or more of its central features.

The TF-notation, for example, makes it particularly obvious that the very same set of operations can generate both senseful and *sinnlos* propositional signs, depending on which propositions one begins with, and the order in which the operations are applied. The truth-table notation, on the other hand, makes it especially apparent that tautology and contradiction are simply "extreme" cases of what can be obtained by the application of the logical operations to meaningful propositions (cf. 4.46). And both notations make clear that propositional signs themselves can be thought of as providing the resources for testing for tautologousness (or contradictoriness) in a mechanical manner.[63] Of course, thanks to Church's theorem, we can now recognize as misplaced Wittgenstein's conviction that this feature could in principle be

---

[63] To check for tautology in the TF-notation one need only check that every "F" occurring as an outer pole traces back to an inconsistent combination of inner poles. The decision procedure in question is described by Wittgenstein in a letter to Russell of November 1913: "One symbolic rule is sufficient to recognize each [truth-functionally valid proposition]: write the proposition down in the ab notation, trace all connections (of poles) from the outside to the inside poles: Then if the b pole is connected to [just] such *groups of inside poles as contain opposite poles of one proposition*, then the whole proposition is a true, logical proposition" (*Letters*, pp. 52–3). (In digesting this remark it helps to bear in mind that "b" here is being thought of as the "F" pole.)

extended to polyadic quantification theory, but Wittgenstein had no particular reason to expect this result.

The virtue of the N-operator notation is that it shows that every proposition can be generated by repeated application of a *single* operator, beginning with elementary propositions. It is also intended to make apparent what singular and general propositions have in common, and wherein they differ. In this notation "p v q" becomes "NN(p,q)" and "∃xFx" becomes "NN(Fx)." What these propositions have in common is the feature of being the results of two applications of the N-operator—the truth-operation that operates on a class of propositions to yield the conjunction of their negations as result. Where they differ is with regard to the manner in which the bases of the first applied operation are given. In the former case they are enumerated, in the latter, they are given as all the values of the propositional function "Fx."[64]

Wittgenstein regards some of these notations as helping to forestall certain philosophical misunderstandings that he takes to be invited by Russell and Whitehead's notation. For example, he sees Russell's notation as encouraging the view that the logical connectives signify by having reference. It is at very least much harder to get this impression from any of Wittgenstein's notations. Speaking of an arbitrarily chosen truth-table, he says:

> It is clear that a complex of the signs "F" and "T" has no object (or complex of objects) corresponding to it, just as there is none corresponding to the horizontal and vertical lines or to the brackets—There are no "logical objects."
> (4.441)

Wittgenstein means that it is apparent to anyone who understands propositions expressed in the truth-table notation that the complex of "T"s and "F"s in the final column is not *intended* to signify by representing an object. The notation itself discourages this interpretation.

Of course, this is not an argument that a truth-table *could* not be construed as containing a sign standing for a logical constant. For one could always view what remains in the truth-table for "pvq" after "p" and "q" have been removed, viz:

| | |
|-----|-----|
| T T | T |
| T F | T |
| F T | T |
| F F | F |

---

[64] I owe this point to Peter Sullivan.

as a typographically elaborate, yet semantically simple, name for the logical object *disjunction*.

The example, however, does bring home just how *unnatural* it would be to read the notation in this way. The natural reading of the truth-table is as expressing a rule for determining the truth-value of the whole proposition from the truth-values of its parts, and perhaps also as conveying that it is this particular truth-functional dependence that constitutes the mode of combination of the constituent propositions.

## [5] THE CONNECTIVES AS OPERATIONS: POSSIBLE ORIGINS OF THE VIEW

We saw earlier that the guiding metaphor informing the *Tractatus'* conception of logic appears to be the summing to zero of oppositely signed magnitudes. In the *Tractatus* this metaphorical conception cohabits with a less figurative one, which—at least on my reconstruction of it—deals directly with propositional signs, Inscriptions and the various operations one may perform on them. But why are the more metaphorical notions associated with the idea of operations upon propositions—i.e. the ideas of reversal and cancellation of senses—so prominent in the *Tractatus*? The answer may be a straightforwardly historical one; for there is reason to think that Wittgenstein's early conceptions of the proposition and of the logical operations may have been significantly molded by his Russellian apprenticeship.

In Russell's *Principles* there is a chapter entitled "Difference of Sense and Difference of Sign" in which Russell discusses the question how to understand signed (i.e. positive and negative) magnitudes (*Principles* §§ 217–223).[65] There he claims that the sign of a magnitude is ultimately owed to what he calls the "sense" of an asymmetric relation. On Russell's view, any asymmetric relation will have a sense that differs from the sense of its converse (*Principles* §219). Thus, in virtue of the difference of sense

---

[65] I am grateful to Thomas Ricketts for first bringing to my attention the fact that Russell speaks of the "sense" of a relation. For a discussion of the relevance of this point in connection with the multiple relation theory of judgement see his "Pictures, Logic and the Limits of Sense," in David. Stern and Hans Sluga eds., *The Cambridge Companion to Wittgenstein*, (Cambridge: Cambridge University Press, 1996), pp. 59–99.

between their constituent relations, the propositions a *is less than*
b and *b is greater than a* are held to be distinct, even though they
are in some sense strongly equivalent (ibid.).

With this idea in place, Russell goes on to explain the notion
of a signed magnitude in terms of the notion of a "stretch":

> A stretch is distinguished from other collections by the fact
> that it consists of all the terms of a series intermediate
> between *two* given terms. (*Principles* § 221)

A stretch can be viewed as a segment of a series of terms ordered
by some transitive, asymmetric relation. Importantly for our purposes, stretches themselves have senses and signs. Russell says:

> By combining the stretch with one sense of the asymmetrical
> relation which must exist between its end-terms, [66] the stretch
> itself acquires sense, and becomes asymmetrical. That is, we
> can distinguish (1) the collection of terms between a and b
> without regard to order, (2) the terms from a to b, (3) the
> terms from b to a. Here (2) and (3) are complex, being com-
> pounded of (1) and one sense of the constitutive relation. Of
> these two, one must be called positive, the other negative.
> (*Principles* § 221)

Russell is saying we can generate two stretches with opposite signs
by combining the terms of a given collection with the different
senses of a given relation.[67] To illustrate this idea, let us consider
some arbitrarily chosen collection of individuals, say: {a, b, c, d}.
From this collection we can form two stretches—(6) aRbRcRd and
(7) $aR^{-1}bR^{-1}cR^{-1}d$—by combining its terms with multiple occur-
rences of the relation R and its converse, respectively. Russell calls
(6) "the *stretch* from a to d" and (7) "the *stretch* from d to a."
Each stretch is a complex with an order imposed on it by *one* sense
of its constituent relation; so a complex formed from a mixture of
a relation and its converse will not count as a stretch. Russell
implies that one of (6) and (7) must be called positive, the other
negative (*Principles* § 221). A magnitude acquires a sign by being
correlated with one or other of the pair of stretches in question.

---

[66] It is not altogether clear whether the end-terms are intended to be constituents of a stretch. The first sentence quoted from § 221 would seem
to suggest not, however, this passage and others would suggest so.
[67] Strictly, Russell ought to say "with a relation and its converse," since
there is no *one* relation that has both of these senses.

We need not delay over the question how this correlation is supposed to be effected, since all that is of immediate interest is the notion of a signed stretch. What it is important to note, however, is that Russell is envisaging the relation in question as obeying the condition usually called "trichotomy": for any x and y in R's field, *exactly one* of xRy, yRx and x=y holds. This condition is implied by the conditions Russell mentions in the course of discussing his "second method" for generating a series: "In this method we have a transitive asymmetrical relation P, and a collection of terms any two of which are such that either xPy or yPx" (*Principles* § 190).

Bearing these points in mind, we can discern several quite striking parallels between these conceptions and certain of Wittgenstein's. First, by trichotomy, if we have a stretch consisting of two distinct terms a and b, then it follows that exactly one of aRb and bRa must obtain. In other words, when a and b are distinct, aRb iff not-bRa. So if we think of propositions on the model of two-termed stretches—which is how Russell tended to think of them in the *Principles*[68]—then negation might be thought of as a matter of reversing a proposition's sense.[69] And, because reversing sense involves reversing sign, we can think of negation as amounting to a reversal of *polarity*. Secondly, Russell goes on in § 222 to link the notion of the sense of a series of spatial points with the idea of a *direction*. He talks of the sense of the stretch as "being indicated by an arrow" (*Principles* § 222).[70] And, as we have seen, in the *Tractatus* the notions of sense and direction are closely linked (3.144 cf. 4.461). Lastly, while stretches have two essential aspects: a non-directed magnitude and a directed sense (to which the sign of this magnitude is owed), Tractarian propositions also have two essential aspects: a non-directed "showing" aspect and a directed "saying" aspect (cf. 3.144 & 4.022).

Given these parallels, it is plausible to suppose that at the time of developing his conception of the logical connectives as opera-

---

[68] In § 53, for example, Russell takes the view that because the copula expresses a relation, all propositions—even those that predicate a simple property of an object—are relational in form.

[69] The model, of course, is no more than suggestive. It breaks down both in explaining what it is for negation to apply to propositions of the form *aRa*, and in dealing with stretches of more than two terms.

[70] This is a link that continues throughout the period relevant to the development of the *Tractatus*. In the 1912 essay "Truth and Falsehood," for example, we find Russell equating sense with direction. See *POP*, p. 73.

tions Wittgenstein was thinking of propositions on the model of a directed (hence signed) stretches.[71] This conjecture would explain the prominence of the "arrow" metaphor in the *Tractatus*, and it would enable us to understand why Wittgenstein came to conceive of the *sinnlosigkeit* of a tautology in terms of the cancellation or summing to zero of senses. Moreover, it would explain how Wittgenstein could have arrived at the view that tautologies and contradictions say nothing, even *before* he had developed the picture theory of the proposition.[72] I would conjecture that the picture theory was developed as a replacement for this conception of the proposition, and that both the explanation of tautology provided by the earlier view and the notion of sense in terms of which it was framed were retained at a metaphorical level.

## [6] LOGIC AS CONTAINING NO SURPRISES

The claim that there are no surprises in logic is made twice in the late sections of the *Tractatus*, different grounds being offered for it on each occasion. At 6.125 Wittgenstein says:

> It is possible, also with the old conception of logic, to give at the outset a description of all "true" logical propositions. (6.125)

> Hence there can *never* be surprises in logic. (6.1251)

Two sections later he says:

> In logic process and result are equivalent [*äquivalent*]. (Hence the absence of surprise.) (6.1261)

In view of their proximity, it would be desirable to have a reading of these two passages that presents them as making the same point, but with slightly different emphases, or, at very least as providing different grounds for the same claim. A further minimal requirement on any satisfactory interpretation is that it should not portray Wittgenstein as denying the obvious. The reading must allow for the undeniable fact that logicians can be surprised about which formulae are derivable in a given system.

---

[71] Frege also discusses the problem of magnitude in *Grundgesetze* II, § 163. However, since he does not employ the notion of *Sinn* in this connection, Russell's work seems the more likely source for these ideas.

[72] Recall that Wittgenstein's first explanation of how a tautology can lack sense without being nonsense occurs in the *Moore Notes* of April 1914, while the picture theory seems to have been developed in September of the same year. (See the relevant entries in the *Notebooks*.)

At first sight Wittgenstein's denial of suprises in logic can seem to be little more than an obvious corollary of his denial that logic has content. If the propositions of logic have no content, then it will be impossible for proofs to provide new information through the reconfiguation of existing content. Wittgenstein's awareness of this point is evident from his drawing a sharp distinction between "proof *in* logic," which merely involves the derivation of tautologies from tautologies by means of rules which preserve tautologousness, and the logical proof of one senseful proposition from others (6.1263).

But, if all Wittgenstein were claiming at 6.125 was that the propositions of logic, being *sinnlos*, do not tell us anything, and so *a fortiori* cannot tell us anything *new*, then we would expect a much simpler ground for the "no surprises" claim than is actually offered. Wittgenstein appeals not to the *sinnlosigkeit* of logic but to the availability "at the outset" of a characterization of all "true" logical propositions (i.e. all tautologies). He implies that such a characterization is provided by his own conception of logic as tautologous, but also by the "old" conception of Frege and Russell. To investigate the sense in which Wittgenstein takes logic to be without surprises, we shall need to begin by asking what kind of logical conception would *fail* to provide for such a characterization "at the outset."

Suppose that one despaired of giving necessary and sufficient conditions for something's being a proposition of logic. How might one nevertheless convey one's conception of logic? One idea would be to state a few simple paradigm cases of logical propositions and then hope that one's audience would be able to "catch on" and extrapolate to future cases from their implicit understanding of what these paradigms have in common. The idea would be to treat the concept of a logical proposition as acquired by abstraction from its instances, in something analogous—but only analogous—to the manner in which, according to certain empiricist accounts, the concept "red" is acquired. Inherent in this idea is the possibility that one's conception of a logical proposition should come to *evolve* as one recognizes new propositions as logical upon proving them within the system.[73] For, in the course of acquiring the concept, certain features common to the initial par-

---

[73] One would be assumed capable of recognizing certain rules of inference as preserving logicality.

adigms might come to be recognized as merely accidental, since not shared by propositions added later to the set. (Think, for example, of the feature of psychological obviousness.) Such a model would present our conception of logic as delivered piecemeal, as successive propositions are established as logical on the basis of certain paradigmatically logical propositions and paradigmatically valid rules of inference. By performing proofs we would be able to learn progressively more about what it is to be a logical proposition. And because there would be no guarantee that our conception would evolve along any foreseeable trajectory, we would, quite possibly, be in for some surprises.

Given that Frege nowhere states adequate necessary and sufficient conditions for something to be a proposition of logic, it is not implausible that Wittgenstein might have viewed him as operating with this kind of conception, although whether he would have been *right* to have done so is a controversial matter upon which I shall not enter here.[74] For our purposes, we need only note that this way of conceiving logic—whether or not it was Frege's way—does provide for "suprises in logic" of a certain kind, namely surprises as to what logic is.

Wittgenstein's own view of logic embodies a rejection of this picture. As we have seen, on his view, we can characterize the notion of tautology in advance of any logical investigation in a way that leaves no room for evolution in our conception: a tautology is simply the result of combining propositions in such a way that their senses sum to zero; less metaphorically, it is a unipolar propositional sign of the same polarity as a propositional sign expressing a true non-logical proposition. On such a conception, there is no room for the idea that proof in logic—i.e. the proof of certain logical propositions from others identified as "axioms"— reveals something about the nature of logic by revealing new kinds of proposition as logical. For apparently distinct tautologies are in fact one and the same propositional sign. (To see that this is so, consider the fact that, for example, "p ∨ ¬p" and "p ∨ ¬¬¬p," are each expressed in the TF-notation by one and the same symbolizing fact, namely, the fact that an appropriately constructed Inscription has only "T"s among its genuine outer poles.) It is for this reason that Wittgenstein, in his more careful moments, speaks

---

[74] That Frege might have thought of logic in this way has been suggested to me by Warren Goldfarb.

not of "tautologies" but of "tautology".[75] But, if we cannot regard the separate lines of a proof as distinct propositional signs, it follows that proof will be powerless to reveal new *kinds* of symbols as belonging to logic.

As 6.125 makes clear, Wittgenstein felt that it was possible to give a characterization of the propositions of logic "from the outset," even from standpoint of the "old" logic of Frege and Russell. To do so, one simply assumes what from a modern perspective amounts to the soundness and deductive completeness of the system in which the proofs are to be given. Having chosen an appropriate system, one may then say that something is a proposition of logic if and only if it can be proved within the system. Wittgenstein's awareness that the systems of Russell and Frege can be employed for this purpose is evident from a remark in the *Moore Notes*:

> We want to say...what properties a symbol must have, in order to be a tautology.

> One way is to give *certain symbols*; then to give a set of rules for combining them; and then to say: any symbol formed from those symbols, by combining them according to one of the given rules, is a tautology. This obviously says something about the kind of symbol you can get in this way.
> This is the actual procedure of [the] *old* Logic: it gives so-called primitive propositions; so-called rules of deduction; and then says what you get by applying the rules to the propositions is a *logical* proposition that you have *proved*. (*Notebooks*, p. 109)

The passage has the puzzling feature that it begins by asking for *necessary* conditions for a symbol to be a tautology and proceeds to offer only *sufficient* ones. But, rather than view this switch as a slip, I believe we ought to regard it as evidence that Wittgenstein is actually offering necessary *and* sufficient conditions for a proposition's being a tautology of the language of a given formal system. Another apparent problem is that, despite Wittgenstein's claim

---

[75] See for example 4.464: "The truth of tautology is certain, of propositions possible, of contradiction impossible," which Wittgenstein explains to Ogden in the following manner:

> Here I have put "tautology" and "contradiction" in the SINGULAR and "proposition" in the *plural* deliberately because there are in fact no contradictions but there is only contradiction, for they all mean the same, i.e. nothing. And the same applies to tautology. (*LO*, p. 30)

that *this* is the procedure of the old logic, what he envisages actually differs from it in an important respect. Whereas for Frege and Russell a proof establishes the truth of the proposition being proved, for Wittgenstein it establishes the fact that the proposition is a tautology. In the *Moore Notes* he writes:

> A so-called *proof* of a logical proposition does not prove its *truth* (logical propositions are neither true nor false) but proves *that* it is a logical proposition = is a tautology. (*Notebooks*, p. 109)

So Wittgenstein puts the old conception of logic to work to yield a characterization of the propositions of logic, but only after it has been substantially reconceived. To be a logical proposition is to be a symbol obtainable from certain tautologous symbols by means of operations that preserve the quasi-syntactic property of tautologousness. ("Quasi-syntactic" because although tautologies can be recognized as such without attending to the senses of their constituents, the conception of tautologies as part of the symbolism makes essential reference to these senses. Far from being purely syntactical items, tautologies are essentially the results (at some remove) of operations on senseful propositions.)

This conception of what it is to be a logical proposition comes to the fore in the *Tractatus* itself:

> Whether a proposition belongs to logic can be calculated by calculating the logical properties of the *symbol*.

> And this we do when we "prove" a logical proposition. For without troubling ourselves about a sense and a meaning, we form the logical proposition out of others by mere *symbolic rules*. (6.126)[76]

Thus, Wittgenstein regards both his own conception of logic and also the axiomatic approaches of Frege and Russell as allowing for the possibility of a specification in advance of any logical investigation of what it is to be a proposition of logic. Because these exhaust the conceptions of logic that Wittgenstein is prepared to

---

[76] The last sentence of 6.126 makes clear that Wittgenstein is envisaging the "rules" in question *not* as the operations by means of which *all* complex propositions are constructed, but as the inference rules of an axiom system.

countenance, he concludes that there can "never" be surprises in logic.

So far, perhaps, so good. But how can this reading be made to fit with 6.1261? How does the "equivalence of process and result"—whatever that means—imply that the concept of a logical proposition is not to be introduced in a way that leaves room for it to evolve? Some light is shed on this question by examining the *Notebooks*. The forerunner of 6.1261 reads:

> In logic (mathematics) process and result are equivalent [*gleichwertig*]. (Hence no surprises). (*Notebooks*, p. 42)

The original idea is that process and result are equivalent in the sense of being *gleichwertig*, which may be translated, literally, as "of equal value." Following this clue, one might read Wittgenstein's remark as asserting that in logic both the set of stages in the proof of a theorem—the process—and the theorem proved—the result—are on an equal footing with respect to their logicality. So understood, the point is essentially that of 6.127:

> All propositions of logic are of equal rank (*gleichberechtigt*); there are not some which are essentially primitive and others deduced from these.

That is to say, there are no propositions whose logicality is owed to their being derivable from other propositions that are, by their very nature, primitively or non-derivatively logical. Rather "Every tautology itself shows that it is a tautology" (6.127). Or, more cautiously, "Logic can always be conceived to be such that every proposition is its own proof" (6.1265). In other words, every tautology provides its own resources for being shown to be a tautology—or at least it does so when framed in a suitable notation. As far as truth-functional logic goes, this is indeed so.[77] As we might now say, every propositional sign in the TF-notation provides us with a decision procedure for checking it for tautologousness: viz. trace the poles. We therefore have a kind of conservativeness result: a proof carried out within an axiom system can tell us nothing about the status of the proposition proved that is not already afforded by a consideration of the proposition as it is in itself. Because we get nothing *more* from an axiom system by way of

---

[77] Again, however, we must recognize that Wittgenstein's attempt to generalize this point to the whole of logic reflects his erroneous commitment to the decidability of first-order quantification theory.

insight into the logicality (or otherwise) of propositions than we already get from the propositions themselves, there is a sense in which there can be no unfolding in our conception of what it is to be a proposition of logic. The equivalence of process and result thus yields the consequence that in logic there are no surprises in the very sense suggested by 6.125.

For Wittgenstein the idea that logic should hold no surprises is a natural corollary of the feature we might describe as its "self-containment." If logical proof is not, as Russell and Frege had supposed, a matter of discovering new general laws about reality, then we lose our most compelling reason to think that our conception of what logic is should be prone to development. This feature of self-containment, the fact that logic does not reach out beyond itself, can be thought of as the unifying theme of the *Tractatus's* account of logic. The mark of the logical is not self-evidence or generality, as (arguably) Frege and Russell had supposed, but the fact that a tautology provides for its *own* verification (6.113).

The *Tractatus's* picture of logic is buttressed by its highly suggestive metaphors, but also, as I have endeavored to show, by its careful choice of notation. It is a powerful conception with something bordering on aesthetic appeal. Wittgenstein himself found the picture so compelling that he thought he had located the true source of our traditional hankering after system:

> Humankind has always had an inkling[79] that there must be a field of questions whose answers—*a priori*—are symmetrical and united into a closed regular structure.
>
> A field in which the proposition, simplex sigillum veri, is valid. (5.4541)

For Wittgenstein this "field" turns out to be the sphere of questions about the nature of *logic*. The answer to these questions is provided by exhibiting the correct logical conception in an appropriate notation. The "closed regular structure" turns out to be, not

---

[79] "Verification" here comes to the idea of calculating the propositional sign's polarity to be the same as that of true senseful propositions. For the reasons we discussed earlier, it cannot be taken to amount to recognizing the proposition as genuinely true.

this or that system of rational metaphysics, but the "infinitely fine network" of "the all-embracing logic which mirrors the world" (5.511).[80]

---

[80] My translation. Here Wittgenstein uses the past participle of the verb "*ahnen.*" Ogden's translation of this verb as "thought" risks making it sound as though Wittgenstein regarded the idea as some kind of delusion. Pears's and McGuinness's translation: "mankind has always had a presentiment," is superior to Ogden's, but a little grandiloquent.

# CHAPTER 2

# Logical Assertion and the Nature of the Proposition

## INTRODUCTION

In the *Tractatus* Wittgenstein makes a number of brief remarks about assertion and its symbolic representation. He describes Frege's assertion sign "⊢" as "logically altogether meaningless" [*bedeutungslos*], and he denies that it belongs to the proposition (4.442). He insists that assertion cannot give a proposition a sense (4.064), and he claims that in Frege and Russell the assertion sign merely shows that these authors hold as true the propositions to which it is affixed (4.442).

It may sound to modern ears as though Wittgenstein is warning against a construal of the assertion sign to which few readers of Frege or Russell would be attracted. To suppose that the assertion sign belongs to the proposition is to regard it as expressing something intrinsic to the thought expressed by the whole sign of which it is a part. And such a view seems both implausible in itself and in tension with the way Frege and Russell explain the sign in their writings.

Russell introduces the assertion sign in *Principia* as showing that a proposition is asserted as true, rather than merely "put forward for consideration."[81] And Frege, who explains the assertion sign as giving expression to a judgement, is consistent in maintaining that a propositional content remains the same whether propounded in a judgement or merely entertained as a supposition.[82]

---

[81] *Principia*, p. 8.
[82] *Begriffsschrift*, §§ 2 & 4, *Grundgesetze* § 5, *Collected Papers*, p. 375; *Gottlob Frege, Posthumous Writings*, Hans Hermes, Friedrich Kambartel and Friedrich Kaulbach eds., trans. Peter Long and Roger White (Oxford: Blackwell, 1980), pp. 177 & 185–6.

Nonetheless, I want to suggest that there is a point to Wittgenstein's warning. The important question is not whether Frege and Russell *intend* the assertion sign to be extrinsic to the vehicle of thought, but whether their philosophical explanations of the proposition entitle them to understand it in this way.

In this chapter I aim to show that both the Frege of the *Begriffsschrift* and the Russell of ca. 1903-05 do indeed give explanations of the proposition which portray the assertion sign as an essential component of the vehicle of thought, and as having something which might fairly be described as a "logical meaning." I will argue that Wittgenstein's early philosophy contains the materials for a philosophically illuminating diagnosis of this error, and that the mistake arises from a genuine incoherence in Frege's and Russell's early conceptions of the proposition. I shall concede, however, that in the *Tractatus* Wittgenstein's critique suffers from being developed only in the context of a dubious reading of Frege's *middle-period* writings.

This last point leads to a second, more methodological, goal of the chapter. There has been a tendency among writers on the *Tractatus* to view Frege as the most important of Wittgenstein's early influences, and to regard the *Tractatus* as the attempt to develop a broadly Fregean philosophy of logic, free from Frege's less palatable commitments.[83] In my view, this assumption is more likely to distort our understanding of the *Tractatus* than to enhance it. For one thing, Wittgenstein is more likely to attack central Fregean notions than to build upon them, for another, his grasp of Frege's philosophy is not nearly so firm as many have supposed. It is this last point that I want to illustrate with reference to the *Tractatus*'s discussion of assertion. I shall argue that much of

---

[83] Examples of this tendency are provided by: James Griffin, *Wittgenstein's Logical Atomism* (Oxford: Oxford University Press, 1964), Peter Geach, "Saying and Showing in Frege and Wittgenstein," in *Essays in Honour of G.H. von Wright*, J. Hintikka ed., *Acta Philosophica Fennica 28* (Amsterdam, 1976); Michael Dummett, "Frege and Wittgenstein" in I. Block, ed. *Perspectives on the Philosophy of Wittgenstein* (Cambridge, Massachusetts: MIT Press, 1981); Gordon Baker, *Wittgenstein, Frege and the Vienna Circle* (Oxford: Blackwell, 1988); Peter Carruthers, *Tractarian Semantics: Finding Sense in Wittgenstein's Tractatus* (Oxford: Blackwell, 1989). I do not mean to suggest that this is more than a tendency. David Pears, for example, attempts to chart some of Russell's influences. See his *The False Prison, A Study in the Development of Wittgenstein's Philosophy, Volume One* (Oxford: Oxford University Press, 1987).

the obscurity in that discussion is owed to Wittgenstein's having read into the middle-period Frege—i.e. the Frege of *Grundgesetze*—certain ideas and conceptions that stem from *Russell*'s work in the period 1900–05.

## [1] KEY TEXTS

The passages of the *Tractatus* that seem to contain the core of Wittgenstein's critique are the following:

> Frege's judgement stroke [*Urteilstrich* (sic)[84]] '⊢' is logically altogether meaningless [*bedeutungslos*]; in Frege (and Russell) it only shows that these authors hold as true the propositions marked this way.

> '⊢' belongs therefore to propositions no more than does the number of the proposition. A proposition cannot possibly assert of itself that it is true. (4.442)

> Every proposition must already have a sense; assertion cannot give it a sense, for what it asserts is the sense itself. And the same holds of denial [*die Verneinung*] etc. (4.064)[85]

> [A proposition without a sense] signifies no thing (truth-value) whose properties are called "false" or "true"; the verb of the proposition is not "is true" or "is false"—as Frege thought—but that which "is true" must already contain the verb. (4.063)[86]

Wittgenstein speaks of Frege's assertion sign as though it were a simple sign, but we should bear in mind that for Frege it is a complex of other signs. In the *Begriffsschrift*, the assertion sign is first introduced as a whole within which we can discern parts. The

---

[84] This is Wittgenstein's mis-spelling of '*Urteilsstrich*'.

[85] Cf. Wittgenstein's *Notebooks* entry for 3rd November 1914: "Only a finished proposition can be negated (And the same holds for all ab-functions)" (My translation), *Notebooks*, p. 25. Because "ab-functions" are operations corresponding to the truth-functional connectives, it seems likely that Wittgenstein's 'etc.' at 4.064 gestures towards the other truth-functional connectives rather than to a range illocutionary acts more comprehensive than assertion and denial.

[86] It is worth mentioning that each of these passages derives from a very early stage in Wittgenstein's work. In fact, each of them occurs, almost identically worded, in the earliest set of notes we have: the *Notes on Logic* of 1913.

parts are assigned different functions: the horizontal stroke '–' is said to combine the signs that follow it into a whole, while the vertical stroke 'I' is said to express an affirmation [*Bejahung*] referring to this whole.[87] In the later *Grundgesetze* the vertical stroke—now called the "judgement stroke"—is still regarded as expressing the act of assertion, but the horizontal stoke—now known as the "horizontal"—is regarded as referring to a function taking the true to the true, and every other object to the false.[88]

Frege is unambiguously identified as Wittgenstein's target at 4.063, so we will begin our investigation by trying to make sense of this passage. First, we should note that the notion of the "verb of the proposition" is not one that figures explicitly in Frege's philosophy. The closest Frege comes to mentioning something that might be thought of as the "verb" is in the *Begriffsschrift*, where he says that his concept-script can be viewed as a language with a "single predicate for all judgements," namely, the assertion sign, read as 'is a fact'.[89] But there are problems with taking the assertion sign, so construed, as the "verb" of 4.063. For one thing, since Frege takes it to be "the single predicate for all judgements," it would be unclear why Wittgenstein should also take 'is false' to be a Fregean "verb."[90] For another, according to 4.063, the verb is supposed to hold or fail to hold of truth-values, while the grammar of 'is a fact' would demand that it holds or fails to hold of something more akin to circumstances or possible states of affairs. Nonetheless, we shall see that there is something to the idea that 'is a fact' functions in the *Begriffsschrift* as "the verb of the proposition" in Wittgenstein's sense, and that this is so even though Wittgenstein is not focusing on the *Begriffsschrift* at 4.063. To see why Wittgenstein might think that there is a notion of "the verb" that includes both 'is a fact,' on the one hand, and 'is true' and 'is false', on the other, it will be necessary to trace the idea of "the verb of the proposition" to its origins, which, I shall argue, are to be found in Russell's discussion of logical assertion in his 1903 *Principles of Mathematics*.[91]

---

[87]   *Begriffsschrift*, § 2.
[88]   *Grundgesetze*, § 5.
[89]   *Begriffsschrift*, § 3.
[90]   This point was first noted by Elizabeth Anscombe, *An Introduction to Wittgenstein's "Tractatus,"* First published 1959, reprinted (Philadelphia: University of Pennsylvania Press, 1971), footnote 1, pp. 105–6.
[91]   We know that Wittgenstein read the *Principles* because he refers to it by name at 5.5351.

## [2] THE "VERB" OF THE PROPOSITION

In the *Principles* Russell seeks to distinguish between a psychological and a logical sense of "assertion." The idea of psychological assertion is relatively simple: it is one of a range of mental acts and attitudes taking propositions as their objects.[91] The idea of logical assertion, on the other hand, is more problematic and does not in the end receive a satisfactory formulation. (I shall argue, in fact, that no such formulation could have been forthcoming, since the notion is ultimately incoherent.)

In the *Principles* Russell sometimes attempts to tie logical assertion closely to truth:

> When a proposition happens to be true, it has a further quality, over and above that which it shares with false propositions, and it is this further quality which is what I mean by assertion in a logical as opposed to a psychological sense.[93]

At other times, he denies that truth is sufficient for logical assertion. He does so because he is reluctant to regard true propositions as logically asserted when they occur as constituents in others.[94]

Perhaps because of his uncertainty over the relevance of truth to logical assertion, Russell also tries to formulate the distinction in a second way, which trades on the difference between expressions such as 'Caesar died', which, as we say, "make an assertion," and those such as 'the death of Caesar', which do not. Russell regards the former expression as expressing a logically asserted proposition, the latter as expressing the same proposition logically unasserted.[95] On this new account, the difference between asserted and unasserted propositions is attributed to the *mode of occurrence* of a privileged constituent known as "the verb." Some texts will help to clarify this idea:

> There appears to be an ultimate notion of assertion, given by the verb, which is lost as soon as we substitute a verbal noun, and is lost when the proposition in question is made the subject of some other proposition.[96]

---

[92] *Principles* § 478.
[93] Ibid., § 52, cf. § 483.
[94] Ibid., § 478.
[95] Ibid., § 52.
[96] Ibid.

Verbs are distinguished by a special kind of connection, exceedingly hard to define, with truth and falsehood, in virtue of which they distinguish an asserted proposition from an unasserted one, e.g. "Caesar died" from "the death of Caesar." [97]

One verb, and one only, must occur as verb in every proposition; but every proposition, by turning its verb into a verbal noun, can be changed into a single logical subject, of a kind which I shall call in future a propositional concept. [98]

To understand what is going on here it is important to realize that for Russell the "verb," the "verbal noun," and the "proposition" are all non-linguistic entities.[99] Russell means that by turning the verb *died* into the verbal noun *death*, one changes the proposition expressed by 'Caesar died' into the "propositional concept" expressed by 'the death of Caesar'. This propositional concept just *is* an unasserted proposition. It is a complex that contains the very same verb as occurs in the asserted proposition, but now in its role "as verbal noun," rather than "as actual verb." [100]

Russell maintains that an unasserted proposition is a complex possessing the "unity" characteristic of propositions.[101] But he is either inconsistent on this point, or else uses "unity" ambiguously,[102] for he also holds that the occurrence of the verb—in its

[97] Ibid., § 46.
[98] Ibid., § 54.
[99] Helpful discussions of Russell's conception of the proposition can be found in Richard Cartwright's essay "On the Origins of Russell's Theory of Descriptions" in his *Philosophical Essays* (Cambridge, Massachusetts: MIT Press, 1987), pp. 95–133, and in chapters 4–6 of Peter Hylton's *Russell, Idealism and the Emergence of Analytic Philosophy*.
[100] *Principles* § 54. §§ 52 & 54 make clear that the very same entity may occur either as verb or as verbal noun.
[101] Ibid., § 54. I am grateful to Thomas Ricketts for calling this passage to my attention.
[102] Ambiguity seems the more likely explanation. In one sense of "unity"(a sense in which even unasserted propositions (i.e. propositional concepts) count as "unities"(a complex is a unity just in case it is not determined by specifying its constituents. For example, if we know that a proposition contains A, B and difference, we do not yet know whether it is the proposition that A differs from B or the proposition that B differs from A. Similarly, this specification of constituents will not suffice to determine whether we have the unasserted proposition "A's difference from B" or "B's difference from A" (ibid., § 135 & § 439). In a narrower sense, something counts as a "unity" only if it is an asserted proposition, i.e. only if it contains the verb in its occurrence "as verb" (ibid., § 54).

role "as verb"— "embodies the unity of the proposition"[103] and this would seem to imply that an unasserted proposition, in which the verb occurs merely "as verbal noun," must lack the unity characteristic of propositions. Furthermore, the theory of "denoting concepts," which Russell articulates in the *Principles*, itself suggests that 'the death of Caesar' should not be regarded as expressing a "proposition" in the strict sense of the term. For, according to this theory, 'the death of Caesar' counts as a "denoting phrase,"[104] and such phrases are supposed to function by expressing, not fully fledged propositions, but propositional *constituents* known as "denoting concepts."[105] So it would be natural to conclude that a so-called "unasserted proposition" does not, after all, have the status of a full proposition, and that 'the death of Caesar' does not express a proposition, but only a denoting concept—one that denotes the fact of Caesar's death. But then it would be appropriate to think of the verb, in its occurrence as verb, as actually completing, and so giving unity to, the propositional complex.

In the *Principles* itself Russell fails to register these consequences of his position, but in the period immediately following its publication he makes remarks that seem to show some awareness of them. In his 1903 manuscript "Dependent Variables and Denotation" he suggests the following explanation of the expression '⊢$p$':

"⊢$p$" expresses "$p$ denotes a fact." [106]

One instance of this would be:

"⊢$p$ The death of Caesar" expresses "*The death of Caesar* denotes a fact,"

---

[103] Ibid.

[104] Denoting phrases include expressions of the form 'the F' 'all Fs' 'any F' 'every F' 'an F' and 'some F', where F signifies what Russell terms a "class-concept,"—i.e. a propositional constituent that yields a propositional function when substituted for the variable u in the propositional function schema: 'x is a u' (ibid., § 58).

[105] Ibid., § 58. Each different kind of denoting concept bears a primitive and indefinable relation of *denoting* to a different kind of object, which object Russell describes as "a kind of combination" of the Fs (ibid., § 62). One denoting phrase, 'the F', expresses a denoting concept that may fail to denote anything at all.

[106] *CP Vol. IV*, p. 304.

where the italicized phrase following the assertion sign *refers* to the denoting concept that is *expressed* by the non-italicized phrase 'the death of Caesar'. To say that *the death of Caesar* denotes a fact is tantamount to saying that Caesar is dead. So on this view both the assertion sign and the English phrase 'denotes a fact' may be regarded as expressing propositional constituents that combine with something non-propositional in nature—viz. a denoting concept—to form a proposition that says the same thing as the asserted proposition expressed by the phrase 'Caesar is dead'.

This proposal, however, must be regarded as a tentative one, for Russell does not arrive at any definite conclusion about how the assertion sign is to be read. In the same manuscript he also tries out the following explanation:

"⊢*p*" expresses "What is denoted by p is true." [107]

Here the assertion sign is presented as saying of a denoting concept that what it denotes is true. But because Russell regards nothing but *propositions* as capable of truth or falsity[108] this seems to commit him to the view that the denoting concept in question denotes a proposition. On the other hand, this may not be a very significant departure from the position we have just considered, for Russell may well have been thinking of facts in this period simply as true propositions.

In his 1905 paper "On Fundamentals" Russell describes the assertion sign as one of the signs of his formalism that occurs "as meaning," by which he means that *what it expresses* occurs in the propositional complex in the peculiar manner necessary to secure propositional unity.[109] The assertion sign therefore signifies a propositional element which, in the terminology of the *Principles*, occurs "as verb." He thus arrives at a view very close to the one

---

[107] Ibid., p. 302.
[108] Ibid., § 52.
[109] Russell writes:

> In every complex, at least one constituent occurs as meaning. It is the constituent occurring as meaning that gives form and unity to the complex; otherwise it would merely be several detached entities. Verbs not in an infinite mood, and prepositions, and conjunctions, when they occur in sentences, normally occur as *meanings*; to make them occur as entities, it is necessary to employ inverted commas or italics. In our symbolic system, '⊃' occurs as meaning; so does '⊢' and '∈'. (*CP Vol. IV*, p. 380.)

criticized in the *Tractatus*[110] for on this account the assertion sign is treated as expressing the verb of the proposition, and so, as functioning as an essential component of the vehicle of thought.[111]

As we shall see, Wittgenstein's criticism of this kind of view is that it simply gives the wrong analysis of the proposition. A proposition does not assert of a denoting concept that it denotes a fact; and more generally, it is not a propositional constituent, logically asserted.[112]

---

[110] Whether Wittgenstein knew of this view of Russell's must remain a matter for conjecture. However it is not unlikely that positions from this period were discussed by Russell and Wittgenstein during the period 1912–13, when teacher and pupil met almost daily to discuss the foundations of logic.

[111] In *Principia*, having introduced the assertion sign in such a way as to suggest that it is extrinsic to the proposition, Russell goes on to make clear that his philosophical view of the nature of the proposition at this time— the so-called "multiple relation theory of judgement"—in fact makes judgement intrinsic to the proposition. In the Introduction he says:

> The phrase which expresses a proposition is what we call an "incomplete symbol"; it does not have meaning in itself, but requires some supplementation in order to acquire a complete meaning. This fact is somewhat concealed by the circumstance that judgement in itself supplies a sufficient supplement, and that judgement in itself makes no *verbal* addition to the proposition. Thus "the proposition 'Socrates is human'" uses "Socrates is human" in a way which requires a supplement of some kind before it acquires a complete meaning; but when I judge "Socrates is human," the meaning is completed by the act of judging, and we no longer have an incomplete symbol. (*Principia*, p. 44)

Russell at this time views judgement as a polyadic relation between the judger and the various entities that Russell formerly took to be elements of the proposition. Because it is now this relation of judgement that secures the unity of the complex, one can think of the assertion sign as expressing something intrinsic to the judgement. However, while such a view is obviously very closely related to the view Wittgenstein is attacking, I doubt that it is his primary target in the passages we are considering. For one thing, because judgement is a psychological relation on this view, it is not clear that the assertion sign could be said to express a "logical meaning." For another, this view is really an *alternative* to the view that the proposition contains an element expressed by the assertion sign, for the primary bearer of truth and falsehood is now not a proposition but a judgement. (This is not to deny, of course, that Wittgenstein attacks this view elsewhere in the *Tractatus*. See, for example, 5.5422.)

[112] This criticism forms part of what Wittgenstein later recognized as a central task of the *Tractatus*: "My object [in the *Tractatus*] was to show the essential difference between a symbol for a proposition and a descriptive phrase." *Lectures* (1932–35), p. 136.

## [3] WITTGENSTEIN'S INTERPRETATION OF FREGE

Using this discussion of Russell as background, I want to turn to a closer examination of the *Tractatus*'s discussion of Frege. It will be simplest if I first state what I take to be Wittgenstein's view, and then turn to a detailed defence of my interpretation. I want to suggest that Wittgenstein sees the Frege of *Grundgesetze* as possessing a conception of the proposition that resembles Russell's 1903–5 view in the following respect: it treats the vehicle for the expression of thoughts as articulated into parts, one of which expresses a propositional element that has the capacity to combine with something non-propositional in nature to yield a proposition. It differs from Russell's view chiefly on a point of terminology: for Wittgenstein's Frege, "the verb" is a privileged linguistic item, rather than what such an item expresses.

In the case of propositions framed in Frege's concept-script, the sign playing the role of "verb" in Wittgenstein's sense is either the assertion sign: '⊢' or its negated counterpart: '⊬'. Thus what Wittgenstein means by a "proposition" at 4.442 is, in effect, what Frege calls a "*Proposition of Begriffsschrift*"[113]—i.e. a sentence of Begriffsschrift immediately preceded by the judgement stroke. Wittgenstein understands such signs, which I shall term 'Propositions', as translatable into English by expressions of the form 'S is true' and 'S is false', where 'S' is replaceable by a sentence of English. So 'is true' and 'is false' can also be said to be "verbs" in a derivative sense.

These verbs are conceived of as each designating a simple property that holds (or fails to hold) of truth-values: the properties, namely, of *being true* and *being false*.[114] Verbs are thus thought of as uniquely applicable simple predicates in the style of Quine's 'Socratizes'.[115] Those ordinary sentences of English that do not contain any verb (in this linguistic, yet non-grammatical, sense) must

---

[113] *Grundgesetze* I, § 5.

[114] The reading can be made to feel less bizarre if we understand *being true* as the property of *being identical with the true*, but we must keep in mind that the predicates are supposed to be *simple*.

[115] See W.V. Quine, *From a Logical Point of View*, second edition (Cambridge, Massachusetts: Harvard University Press, 1953), pp. 7–8, & *Word and Object* (Cambridge, Massachusetts: MIT Press, 1960), p. 176 ff.

be thought of as abbreviations of their verb-containing counter-parts,[116] for only the latter exhibit the articulation essential to propositions (cf. *4.032*).

This, then, is a sketch of the bare bones of the view that I want to claim Wittgenstein attributed to Frege. I believe it enables us to explain much of what Wittgenstein says at *4.442*, *4.063* and *4.064*.[117] To make this plausible it will help to spell out the views that Wittgenstein would seem to be *attacking* in these passages. They are six in number:

1) The assertion sign[118] '⊢' belongs to the proposition itself (*4.442*).

2) The assertion sign is logically meaningful; it has a logical pur-pose or role (*4.442*).[119]

3) Some propositions assert their own truth (*4.442*).

4) Assertion gives a proposition a sense; a proposition has no sense prior to being asserted (*4.064*).

5) The verb of each proposition is either 'is true' or 'is false' (*4.063*).

6) There can be sentences without sense that refer to things (truth-values) whose properties are called 'true' or 'false' (*4.063*).

---

[116] The natural language verb-containing counterpart of 'Caesar is dead' would be 'Caesar is dead is true'.

[117] Although I believe this account explains the uses of 'proposition' at *4.442*, *4.064* and *4.063*, it should be noted that Wittgenstein is also happy to speak of names of truth-values as Fregean "propositions." See, for example, *5.02*.

[118] Throughout I shall use the expression 'the assertion sign' to refer to this sign. Frege, however, did not himself use any technical term for this sign, which he merely viewed as a complex of others.

[119] Although Wittgenstein describes the sign as "*logisch ganz bedeutungs-los*" he does not seem to mean by this that the sign lacks a *Bedeutung* in Frege's technical sense of the term. Rather, he calls a sign "*logisch bedeu-tungslos*" simply when in an ordinary sense it serves no purpose (cf. *5.47321*). That being so, we shall nonetheless see that *in this instance* it is precisely *because* the sign lacks a *Bedeutung* in Frege's technical sense that Wittgenstein takes it to lack one in the ordinary sense.

Of these theses only (5) is expressly attributed to Frege. However, the attribution of thesis (2) to Frege (and possibly to Russell) is plausibly implied, as, given the "therefore" of 4.442, is the attribution of thesis (1). We have grounds to think that thesis (6) is also intended to be attributed to Frege, both in view of its reference to the Fregean notion of a "truth-value" and because of its setting in 4.063. It is less clear what we ought to say about theses (3) and (4).

On my reading of the view Wittgenstein is aiming to criticize, thesis (1) is explained by the fact that the assertion sign figures—either negated or on its own—in every complex of signs that constitutes a Proposition of Begriffsschrift, and so, as Wittgenstein puts it, "belongs" to the proposition (i.e. Proposition) itself. Thesis (2) is explained by the assertion sign's having the logical role of combining with a mere name of a truth-value to yield a Proposition. Thesis (4)—that assertion bestows a sense on an otherwise senseless sign—also squares with this view, or at least it does so on the Tractarian assumption that names cannot have senses (cf. 3.3), for it is only with the introduction of the assertion sign or its negated counterpart (or their English equivalents 'is true' and 'is false') that a name of a truth-value comes to have the logical articulation required of a genuine proposition (4.032). How my reading explains (5) and (6) is obvious from what has been said already. This leaves only thesis (3), which it will be convenient to consider later on.

## [4] ANSCOMBE'S UNDERSTANDING OF THE "VERB"

I shall turn in a moment to defending my attribution to Wittgenstein of this reading of Frege, but first I want to consider a rival interpretation of Wittgenstein's understanding of the "verb" that has been proposed by Elizabeth Anscombe. In her *Introduction to Wittgenstein's 'Tractatus'*,[120] Anscombe suggests that the verbs 'is true' and 'is false' should be understood as Wittgenstein's natural-language renderings of the horizontal of *Grundgesetze* and the negation sign: '⊤' respectively.[121] Her view has a certain plausibility because the horizontal can be read as meaning "is identical with the true." There are, however, reasons for doubting that this is what Wittgenstein has in mind.

---

[120] Anscombe, G. E. M. *An Introduction to Wittgenstein's Tractatus* (Philadelphia: University of Pennsylvania Press, 1959).
[121] Anscombe, loc. cit.

First, if Anscombe is right, and Wittgenstein's target is *not* the view that the *assertion sign* plays the role of verb of the proposition, then we forfeit our explanation of thesis (1). It remains a mystery why Wittgenstein should have regarded the assertion sign as belonging to the proposition. And, significantly perhaps, Anscombe is silent on this point.

Secondly, when discussing Frege in the *Tractatus* or the *Notebooks* Wittgenstein says nothing to suggest that he recognizes Frege's horizontal as a sign in its own right; and, as we have seen, he inaccurately terms the whole assertion sign, rather than just its vertical part, the "*Urteilsstrich*" (4.442). These facts suggest Wittgenstein may not have grasped the purpose of the horizontal, perhaps regarding it as a semantically insignificant part of the assertion sign.[122]

Some support for this idea can be gleaned from 4.43 where, after suggesting that Frege was right to employ truth-conditional explanations of the connectives of his Begriffsschrift as a starting point, Wittgenstein goes on to express a reservation:

> Only Frege's explanation of the truth-concept is false: if "the true" and "the false" were really objects and were the arguments in ¬p etc., then Frege's determination of the sense of "¬p" would be no determination at all.[123] (4.431)

The argumentative structure of this passage is clear: if truth is to play a role in specifying the senses of logically complex expressions

---

[122] We can appreciate how Wittgenstein might have come to think that it was the assertion sign rather than the vertical stroke that marked something as an assertion; for Frege himself first introduces the assertion sign in a way that is apt to give this impression. In § 2 of *Begriffsschrift* he writes:

> A judgement will always be expressed by means of the sign '⊢', which stands to the left of the sign, or combination of signs, indicating the content of the judgement.

Here it certainly seems as though the *whole* assertion sign is being assigned the function of expressing a judgement. And, indeed, in the same section Frege goes on to say that the horizontal part of *this sign* is to be known as the content stroke, which would convey the impression that the horizontal stroke attached in the first instance to the vertical stroke rather than to the sentence expressing the proposition's content.

[123] My translation. Here I am guided by *PT*, 4.4221, where Wittgenstein makes it plain that in the envisaged circumstances Frege's "determination" would be unworthy of the name.

then Frege will have to explain the truth-concept otherwise than as an object. For, if it is so understood, his stipulations of sense for the logical constants will be rendered inadequate.[124]

What is unclear is why conceiving of truth and falsity as objects is supposed to have these dire consequences. Why is Frege's determination of sense "no determination at all"? There is a natural reading of this passage that provides a straightforward answer to this question, but which suggests that Wittgenstein failed to grasp the intended role of the horizontal. It is this: by understanding truth and falsity as two objects among others, Frege has rendered his stipulations incapable of determining the truth-value of (say) '¬p' in the event that 'p' refers to some object other than a truth-value. But it was in order to handle precisely this difficulty that Frege first introduced the horizontal. When 'p' is a name of some object other than a truth value '—p' is a name of the false; so, because negation always applies to propositions that are preceded by the horizontal, Wittgenstein's problem does not arise. His finding a difficulty here suggests that he failed to appreciate the horizontal's intended role.

To be sure, these considerations do not amount to a knockdown argument against Anscombe's reading, but, in my view, they cast enough doubt on it to make an alternative seem attractive.[125]

## [5] DEFENCE OF MY INTERPRETATION

I will now defend my attribution to Wittgenstein of the reading of Frege outlined above, both by citing some further direct evidence and by explaining how the reading might naturally have

---

[124] By contrast, Anscombe sees the argument of this passage as running as follows: "Frege's specifications fail to determine a sense for '¬p' because on Frege's own principles you do not specify a sense by specifying a reference" (Anscombe, op. cit., p. 107). I believe this interpretation makes too much of an accidental feature of Wittgenstein's presentation. What is at issue is not whether the sense of a *proposition* can be determined by specifying its reference (of course, it cannot), but rather whether Frege's stipulations for the negation sign are sufficient to determine the sense of '¬p' *given that the sense of 'p' is already determined*. Thus what is really in question is whether the stipulations determine a sense for the negation sign. What misleads us is that Wittgenstein is prevented from framing the question in this way because he construes the negation sign as a sign for an operation rather than a functional expression with a sense of its own (cf. 3.3 & 5.25).

[125] I discuss another advantage my reading has over Anscombe's in section 7 of this chapter.

suggested itself to Wittgenstein given Frege's own remarks in *Grundgesetze*. To avoid long-windedness, I will label the conception of assertion I see Wittgenstein as having attributed to Frege "the attributed view," and the thesis that Wittgenstein attributed this view to Frege "the attribution thesis." Our best evidence for the attribution thesis is contained in 4.063—a passage that is important enough to warrant a full quotation:

> An illustration to explain the concept of truth. A black spot on white paper; the form of the spot can be described by saying of each point of the plane whether it is white or black. To the fact that a point is black corresponds a positive fact: to the fact that a point is white (not black), a negative fact. If I indicate [*bezeichne*] a point of the plane (a truth-value in Frege's terminology), this corresponds to the assumption [*Annahme*] proposed for judgement, etc. etc.
>
> But to be able to say that a point is black or white, I must first know under what conditions a point is called white or black; in order to be able to say "p" is true (or false) I must have determined under what conditions I call "p" true, and thereby I determine the sense of the proposition.
>
> The point at which the analogy breaks down is this: we can indicate a point on the paper, without knowing what white and black are; but to a proposition without a sense corresponds nothing at all, for it signifies no thing (truth-value) whose properties are called "false" or "true"; the verb of the proposition is not "is true" or "is false"—as Frege thought— but that which "is true" must already contain the verb.

If we work through this passage carefully, we will see that the view being attacked—which Wittgenstein takes to be Frege's view of truth—actually amounts to the attributed view.

Wittgenstein's strategy is to show that the analogy on which he takes the view to be based goes lame at a key point. The first paragraph introduces the analogy. We can set out the relevant correspondences as follows:

| | |
|---|---|
| The paper | The world |
| The form of the spot | The way the world is |
| A point on the plane | A Fregean truth-value |
| A description of the spot | A description of the world |
| The fact that a point is black | A positive fact |
| The fact that a point is not black | A negative fact |
| The indication of a point on the plane | An assumption proposed for judgement |

Before proceeding, I ought to say a word about what Wittgenstein means by an "assumption" [*Annahme*] in this context. For the time being I will be dogmatic:[126] it is simply something linguistic, namely a *whole* name of a truth-value, by which I mean a proper name such as '—*A*' or:

But not one of the proper names occurring as components within these. (One qualification: because it seems likely that Wittgenstein failed to recognize the horizontal as a sign in its own right, we should actually think of the *Annahme* as a whole name of a truth-value in the sense just explained, but *minus* the initial horizontal.)

The key idea of the first paragraph is that the designation[127] of a point corresponds in the analogy to the designation of a truth-value by means of the *Annahme*, where the *Annahme* is thought of as something merely "proposed for judgement."[128] In the geometri-

---

[126] I argue for this view in section 8 of this chapter.

[127] I have decided to understand the word 'indicate' in the first paragraph as a stylistic variant of 'designate' for two reasons. First, the use of 'indication' to mean 'designation' has a precedent in Russell's choice of the former term to translate Frege's '*Bedeutung*' (*Principles*, § 476); secondly, the corresponding passage from the *Notes on Logic*, itself a translation by Russell from Wittgenstein's original manuscript, has 'designate' where the *Tractatus* has 'indicate' (See *Notebooks*, p. 99).

[128] In the *Notes on Logic* Wittgenstein puts the point by saying that to express a proposition without the judgement stroke is "to set up an assumption to be decided upon" (*Notebooks*, p. 99).

cal case we designate a point in order to go on and say of it that it is black (or white); so maintaining the analogy will demand that we think of judgement as a matter of *predicating* one or other of the properties introduced by 'is true' and 'is false' of the designation of the *Annahme* (i.e. of a truth-value).

The second paragraph is *not* a continuation of the analogy.[129] Rather, it presents Wittgenstein's own views about what it is to have a grasp of the notion of truth. To have a grasp of truth is to know what it is for truth to apply to a proposition. And to know what it is for truth to apply to a *particular* proposition is to grasp that proposition's sense. This idea is operative in the reasoning of the third paragraph, which shows how the analogy breaks down.

The disanalogy consists in this: we can single out a point without knowing what black and white are, for we can make use of the co-ordinates of the plane. However, we cannot single out a particular truth-value without grasping the notions of truth and falsity. Why not? Well, what would provide the analogue of a co-ordinate system in the semantic case? All that would seem to be available are the various propositions themselves. Could we make use of them to secure reference to a truth-value by means of a description of the form 'the truth-value of such-and-such a proposition'? By no means. For in order to use such a description we should need some way of specifying a proposition that made no use of the notions of truth or falsity. Yet, to specify a proposition[130] we should need to specify its sense.[131] That is, we should need to state the conditions under which it is true (4.024). But a grasp of these conditions involves a grasp of truth, so we should not have by-passed our reliance on this concept after all.

---

[129] To sustain the analogy, truth and falsity would have to be applicable to truth-values, not propositions. So if we were to read this paragraph as continuing the presentation of the analogy, we should have to judge that the analogy had *already* broken down. However, the third paragraph indicates that the analogy is meant to break down at a different point.

[130] Wittgenstein means by a "proposition" in this context something answering to *his* conception of the proposition, namely a "propositional sign in its projective relation to the world" (3.12).

[131] This claim reflects a commitment to the view that we can specify a proposition only by presenting it, so to speak, transparently, that is to say, in such a way that given the presentation one is immediately in a position to grasp the proposition specified. Such is not the case, for example, in designations of propositions such as: 'The fifth postulate of Euclid'.

The analogy thus fails: we cannot think of truth and falsity as properties of truth-values, as black and white are properties of points on a page. And in rejecting this conception we thereby also reject the idea that propositions may be thought of as mere names of truth-values, names that might—for all their capacity to function as names is concerned—express no thought whatsoever: "to a proposition without sense corresponds nothing at all, for it signifies no thing (truth-value) whose properties are called 'false' or 'true'." Judgement is therefore not to be understood on the model of predication, and the assertion sign (consequently) is not to be thought of as introducing a property.

Because Frege is clearly identified at 4.063 as the proponent of the view being criticized here, this passage furnishes some direct evidence for the attribution thesis: some indirect evidence for the thesis emerges from a consideration of *how* Wittgenstein might have been steered towards this reading by some of Frege's own remarks.

## [6] FREGE'S MISLEADING REMARKS

Let us begin by considering how Frege introduces the assertion sign in *Grundgesetze*.[132] He writes:

> In a mere equation there is as yet no assertion: '2+3=5' only designates a truth-value, without its being said which of the two it is....We therefore require another sign in order to be able to assert something as true. [133]

The point Frege wants to make is that the *thought* expressed by '2+3=5' does not assert itself; rather, *we* have to intervene by recording our recognition that the proposition is true, and we do this *not* by writing 'It is true that 2+3=5', which would merely express the same unasserted thought, but by making a judgement and expressing this *judgement* by means of the assertion sign.

Frege's point is thus that the expression '2+3=5' designates a truth-value in contrast to expressing a judgement. He is *not* claiming that '2+3=5' designates a truth-value in contrast to *expressing a sense*. I think it likely, however, that Wittgenstein read this pas-

---

[132] The relevance of *Grundgesetze* to Wittgenstein's reading is suggested by his use of '*Urteilsstrich*' at 4.442, a term that is absent from *Begriffsschrift*.

[133] *Grundgesetze* I, § 5.

sage in the second of these ways, not because it obviously suggests
such a reading when taken alone, but because it may seem to do so
when read in conjunction with the following passage, which
occurs a few pages earlier:

> ...I do not mean to assert anything if I merely write down an
> equation, but...I merely designate a truth-value, just as I do
> not assert anything if I merely write down '$2^2$', but merely
> *designate* a number.[134]

By drawing an analogy between names of truth-values and complex numerals, Frege might seem to be suggesting that these
expressions are alike in failing to express complete thoughts,
rather than alike in failing to express judgements. The two passages thus work in tandem to create the impression that the assertion sign is invoked to enable a mere name to do linguistic work of
an appropriately fact-presenting kind.[135]

Some of Frege's glosses of Propositions of Begriffsschrift might
also have helped Wittgenstein to read him in the way I am suggesting. Consider, for example, the following:

$$\vdash\!\!\!\!\top\qquad 2^2 = 5$$

in words: $2^2 = 5$ is not the True.[136]

The gloss may seem to suggest that the negated assertion sign has
a content that can be read as 'is not the True', which might in turn
be seen as a mere notational variant of the verb 'is false'. (The suggestion is, of course, misleading: Frege would have regarded the
assertion sign as indicating assertoric force and the negation sign
as contributing to the sense of the sentence asserted.)

A third factor is Frege's tendency to want to claim a *special*
status for the judgement stroke. In *Grundgesetze* he writes:

---

[134] Ibid., § 2.
[135] I owe this formulation to Warren Goldfarb.
[136] Ibid., § 6.

> The judgement stroke I reckon neither among the *names* [of Begriffsschrift] nor among the *marks*; it is a sign of its own special kind. [137]

In "Funktion und Begriff" we learn the nature of the sign's peculiarity:

> The judgement stroke [*Urteilsstrich*] cannot be used to construct a functional expression; for it does not serve, in conjunction with other signs, to designate an object. '⊢2+3 = 5' does not designate anything: it asserts something. [138]

The assertion sign is thus distinguished from (nearly[139]) all other signs of Begriffsschrift by its ability to combine with names of truth-values in such a way as to yield a saturated expression that is not another name. This way of characterizing the assertion sign is strongly suggestive of the attributed view, for if—as Wittgenstein actually believed—being a name disqualifies an expression from expressing a thought, then a Begriffsschrift designed for the expression of thoughts will need to contain a sign that combines with a name of a truth-value to form, not another name, but an articulated sign capable of expressing a thought. The characterization given above would present the assertion sign as ideally suited to this task.

## [7] THE ROLE OF WITTGENSTEIN'S PHILOSOPHY OF LOGIC

There is, then, much in Frege's writings to invite the reading I have termed "the attributed view." Moreover, Frege's remarks are especially suggestive when read against the background of Wittgenstein's own philosophy of logic. By 1913 Wittgenstein had already arrived at the idea that every genuine proposition is "bipolar"—i.e. essentially either-true-or-false.[140] By contrast, Frege's view—that the relation between a proposition and its truth or falsity is one of naming—makes it seem a lucky accident that every proposition turns out to be either true or false (cf. 6.*111*).

---

[137] *Principles,* § 26.
[138] My translation. The translators of Frege's *Collected Papers* have "assertion sign." "Funktion und Begriff," 22, footnote 7. Reprinted in Funktion, Begriff, Bedeutung. Fünf logische Studien, ed. Günther Patzig, second edition (Göttingen, 1966).
[139] Frege's sign for definition also has this feature.
[140] *Notebooks,* pp. 94–5 & 98–99.

A related criticism is the one I alluded to in my discussion of the "illustration" of *4.063*: Frege's view makes it seem as though the bearer of truth and falsity can be true or false quite independently of being something with the capacity to present facts. A symptom of this feature of Frege's logic is the presence in *Begriffsschrift* of names of truth-values that cannot be thought to convey that anything is the case. An example would be: "$\grave{\varepsilon}(—\varepsilon)$', the name of the value-range stipulated to be identical with the true.[141]

Bearing these problems in mind, it is not hard to imagine Wittgenstein reaching the conclusion that Frege's assertion sign was introduced in the hope—already a forlorn one given Frege's assimilation of propositions to names—of restoring to the proposition its fact-presenting aspect, and with this its essential bipolarity.[142] That is to say, one can imagine Wittgenstein thinking of the assertion sign and its negated counterpart as intended to introduce properties, one or other of which is supposed to hold of every truth-value. And because these "properties" would not be functions from objects to truth-values, we can imagine him thinking of the sign that introduces them as intended to combine with a name of a truth-value to yield something which, unlike a name, has genuine propositional articulation.

Incidentally, these considerations provide a third reason for preferring the assertion sign to the horizontal as the candidate for Frege's supposed "verb." The horizontal does not even *begin* to look like something that could restore to a name of a truth-value the fact-presenting aspect appropriate to a genuine proposition. The horizontal combines with a proper name to yield *another* proper name. So if Wittgenstein had regarded *Grundgesetze*'s treatment of sentences of Begriffsschrift as *names* as the problem prompting the introduction of the verb, he could scarcely have regarded the horizontal as its intended solution.

## [8] THE "ANNAHME"

I want now to defend my reading of the term "*Annahme*" as it occurs in the *Tractatus*. As Anscombe notes, Wittgenstein's ten-

---

[141] *Grundgesetze* I, § 10.
[142] This observation was first made by Max Black. *A Companion to Wittgenstein's "Tractatus"* (Ithaca, New York: Cornell University Press, 1964), p. 227.

dency to treat this Meinongian term as expressing a technical notion in Frege's philosophy appears to derive from Russell's similar treatment of it in the *Principles*.[143] Russell identifies the *Annahme* with what he terms "the truth-value of a *Gedanke*" and by this he means not what we, or Frege, would mean, but rather a whole sentence of Begriffsschrift preceded by the horizontal stroke.[144] Anscombe conjectures that this was also how Wittgenstein regarded it.[145]

I agree with Anscombe that for Wittgenstein the *Annahme* is to be treated as a whole unasserted proposition, since that much is apparent from his description of it at 4.063 as something *proposed* for judgement. And I agree that it must be something linguistic, since in the last paragraph of 4.063 Wittgenstein's envisaged target is the view that the bearer of truth or falsity (i.e. the *Annahme*) is something with the status of a *sinnlos name*. I cannot, however, go along with Anscombe's identification of the *Annahme* with a sentence of the form '—A', for, as I have already argued,[146] it seems likely that Wittgenstein regarded the horizontal as an intrinsic part of the assertion sign rather than as attaching to what gets asserted.

## [9] AN ALTERNATIVE DIAGNOSIS

Wittgenstein arrived at the *Tractatus*'s criticisms of Frege's assertion sign very early in his career. In fact, these views were formulated, much as we find them in the *Tractatus*, in the 1913 *Notes on Logic*. These notes were written about a year before Wittgenstein formulated his so-called "picture theory" of the proposition and roughly six months before the first appearance of the theme of "showing" in Wittgenstein's philosophy, in the *Moore Notes* of April 1914. It seems likely that Wittgenstein re-examined the issue of assertion in the light of these new developments. For in the *Notebooks* entries from late 1914 and early 1915 he considers an alternative, or perhaps complementary, diagnosis of Frege's appeal to the assertion sign. In the *Notebooks* entry for January 11th, 1915 he writes:

> A yardstick does not say that an object that is to be measured is one yard long.

---

[143] Anscombe, op. cit., p. 105, note 1.
[144] *Principles*, § 477.
[145] Anscombe, op. cit. pp. 105–6 n. 1.
[146] See section 4 of this chapter.

Not even when we know that it is supposed to serve for the measurement of this *particular object*.
Could we not ask: What has to be added to that yardstick in order for it to assert something about the length of the object? (The yardstick without this addition would be the 'assumption' [*Annahme*].)[147]

Clearly, the purpose of this passage is to suggest an analogy between the yardstick and the *Annahme*: the *Annahme*, like the yardstick, is by itself incapable of asserting anything, but one might easily get the impression that the yardstick or *Annahme* may nevertheless come to say something, if provided with the right kind of supplementation. The implication of the passage is that in each case it is equally misguided to hope to find some such addition. The passage is of interest because it seems highly plausible that in the case of the *Annahme* the envisaged "addition" is the assertion sign.

It is important to note that around this time Wittgenstein appears to have changed his way of understanding the *Annahme*. In the *Notebooks* entry for the 12th of November 1914 he writes:

Then is the picture perhaps not the simple proposition, but rather its proto-picture [*Urbild*] which must occur in it?[148]

Then this proto-picture is not actually a proposition (though it has the form [*Gestalt*] of a proposition) and *it* might correspond to Frege's 'assumption' [*Annahme*][149]

Wittgenstein's emphasis on the impersonal pronoun in the second sentence appears to signal his realization that he has hit upon a new possibility for understanding the "*Annahme.*" The comparison with the proto-picture suggests that Wittgenstein is now thinking of the *Annahme* as something that bears a merely *specious* resemblance to a proposition, a resemblance that is founded in the *Annahme*'s purporting to answer to the "picturing" aspect of a genuine proposition. I will develop the Yardstick passage's implicit

---

[147] *Notebooks*, pp. 37–8.
[148] I have chosen to render '*Urbild*' uniformly as 'proto-picture' in preference to following Anscombe's oscillation between this translation and 'prototype'.
[149] Ibid, p. 29. Emphasis Wittgenstein's, translation my own. Note that the stress on 'it' is missing from Anscombe's translation.

criticism of this idea more fully below, but for now the important point to note is that it represents a shift of emphasis from the criticisms of the 1913 *Notes on Logic*, where Wittgenstein's dissatisfaction with the *Annahme* centred upon its having the status of a *name*. I will argue that this shift in Wittgenstein's conception of the *Annahme* is the correlate of a new way of thinking of Frege's assertion sign: namely as something that expresses the actualization of a state of affairs. Since such an interpretation can plausibly be seen as picking up on Frege's remarks about the assertion sign in the *Begriffsschrift*, I will briefly turn to this work before examining the Yardstick passage in more detail.

## [10] THE ASSERTION SIGN IN THE BEGRIFFSSCHRIFT

Throughout the *Begriffsschrift* what I have been calling "the assertion sign" is referred to by Frege only as "the sign '⊢'." What remains after the judgement stroke is omitted (viz. '—A') is said to express something that may be paraphrased as "the circumstance [*Umstand*] that A" or as "the proposition [*Satz*] that A."[150] Frege later expressed dissatisfaction with these early characterizations, and with good reason, for they plainly possess different "grammars": whereas propositions are true or false, circumstances are actual or non-actual.

The situation is thus already quite complicated even before Frege goes on in section 3 to suggest a way in which '⊢A' might be cashed. The suggestion occurs in the course of a passage where Frege is stressing the relative lack of importance for his system of various traditional logico-grammatical classifications, such as that of subject and predicate. He argues that we may, if we wish, retain the subject/predicate distinction simply by choosing to regard *Begriffsschrift* as a language in which '⊢' plays the role of the "common predicate for all judgements." To view the assertion sign in this way would, he implies, involve analogizing Begriffsschrift to an imaginary language in which every proposition is expressed by a sentence consisting of an appropriately complex noun-phrase— e.g. 'the violent death of Archimedes at the capture of Syracuse'— and the predicate 'is a fact'.[151] It is not clear how seriously Frege

---

[150] Note that '*Satz*' is thus used differently in the *Begriffsschrift* and *Grundgesetze*, since in the latter work it is used for a sentence *together with* the assertion sign.

intends us to take this remark, which may merely be a concession to those who wish to treat every proposition as having subject-predicate form, but if we were to take it seriously, we could easily arrive at one or other of the following views as to how the expression '⊢A' is to be understood—which one, depending on whether we saw the assertion sign or just the judgement stroke as playing the role of "common predicate for all judgements":

> A) '⊢' has a content expressible in the words 'the circumstance that . . . is a fact', where the ellipsis is filled with a sentence, A, which is thought of as picturing or showing a possible situation, but not as designating one. On this reading '—' functions as a singular-term-forming operator, while '|' functions as the predicate 'is a fact'.

> B) '⊢' has a content expressible in the words 'is a fact'; and A is a singular term *designating* a possible situation (e.g. 'the violent death of Archimedes at the capture of Syracuse').

It is not clear to what extent Frege was aware of the differences between these characterizations, and it would be rash to suppose that he regarded either one of them as uniquely correct when the *Begriffsschrift* went to press. For our purposes, however, all that matters is that, on either reading, the assertion sign can be understood as attaching to a sentence that introduces a possible situation *as a mere possibility*—i.e. without saying that it obtains. On both readings it is thus possible to view the assertion sign as the extra element needed to enable the *Annahme* to express a thought. With this in mind, let us return to the 'Yardstick' passage.

## [11] THE YARDSTICK PASSAGE

Wittgenstein begins by drawing our attention to a fact about how a yardstick does *not* operate: it is not characteristic of a yardstick to represent objects as being one yard in length—not even when the particular object to be measured is known. This point is familiar and unexceptionable. The yardstick does not make its own judgements of length, it facilitates *ours*, by showing how long an object one yard long would have to be.[152]

The function of the yardstick is to mark out a length that objects *could* have. In virtue of this function, the salient feature of

---

[151] *Begriffsschrift* § 3.
[152] I shall proceed on the assumption that Wittgenstein's analogy involves the simplifying assumption that the yardstick has no graduating lines.

the yardstick (considered outside of any particular context) is its length. Thus by its very nature the yardstick (considered by itself) renders salient a certain length. Accordingly, we can get the feeling—at least I take it that this is Wittgenstein's point—that it somehow *gestures towards* a particular length; and, gripped by this feeling, we can come to think of the yardstick as, so to speak, "half-way" towards saying something. That is, we can get the feeling that all that would be needed to render the yardstick articulate is the addition of a sign to indicate that its length is exemplified in something else. The addition, perhaps, of an utterance—in the presence of the yardstick, and accompanied by the appropriate pointing gesture—of the following sentence: 'The object to be measured is *this* long'. Of course, this idea is confused, for it would not now be the yardstick that said something, but the whole utterance together with its reference to the yardstick.

The purpose of the Yardstick passage is to draw our attention to what Wittgenstein sees as an analogous illusion in the case of the *Annahme*. As Wittgenstein thinks of it, the *Annahme* is supposed merely to indicate one possible situation (one point in logical space), while remaining neutral on the question whether or not this situation is actual. So conceived, it can seem to stand in need of something extra to register that the situation presented is presented as being actually, and not merely possibly, the case. Precisely what one is inclined to choose for this addition will depend on how the *Annahme* is supposed to function. If we envisage it as somehow showing, or picturing a possible situation, we might choose something with the sense of the following locution: 'The situation depicted by this sign: "..." is a fact'.[153] (The ellipsis being filled by the *Annahme*.) If, on the other hand, the *Annahme* is understood as *designating* a possible situation, then we might choose the predicate: 'is a fact'. On the first of these ways of thinking, the addition would turn out to resemble the assertion sign of the *Begriffsschrift* under construal (A); while on the second, it would resemble the same sign under construal (B).

The "Yardstick" passage can thus be viewed as offering a new diagnosis of Frege's introduction of the assertion sign; and along with it, an implied criticism. The criticism comes in two versions,

---

[153] Cf. the *Notebooks* entry for November 1st, 1914: "Analogy between proposition and description: *The complex which* is congruent with this sign" (*Notebooks*, p. 23).

depending on whether the *Annahme* is understood according to (A) or (B). Against (A) the charge is that the perceived need for the assertion sign is rooted in a confused view of the *Annahme*'s representational capacities. The *Annahme* masquerades as something that is capable of showing, picturing or presenting a possible situation, while not expressing that that situation obtains. However, it is quite unclear how any sign could *present* a possible situation unless it *already* expressed a proposition. The problem is manifested symbolically by the fact that it only makes sense to replace the ellipsis in (A) with expressions that already say something. The assertion sign is thus intrinsically otiose: when it can be "added" to something, the result is only a more wordy formulation of the proposition already expressed.

Against (B) the argument has a slightly different structure. Now the *Annahme* is supposed to function as a name of a situation. The problem is that it can function in this way only if it already contains a proposition. The *Annahme* would have to be some expression such as 'the circumstance that p'. But again this expression could only pick out a situation if 'p' were already a proposition that represented the situation as obtaining. But then the *Annahme* could not be something preliminary to a fully formed proposition, for it would presuppose the very proposition whose preliminary form it was supposed to be.

As it stands, this argument is not decisive, for one might reply that the expression naming the situation could be of the form 'the circumstance of $\Phi$-ing' where $\Phi$ is a verbal noun. An example would be: 'the circumstance of opposite poles attracting'. But it is plausible that we can only grasp expressions of this form because we understand them as transforms of expressions of the form: 'the circumstance that p,' where 'p' expresses a proposition—in this case, the sentence: 'Opposite poles attract'.

At 4.022 Wittgenstein says that:[154]

> The proposition *shows* how things stand, *if* it is true. And *says that* they do so stand.

What I have said so far suggests that Wittgenstein would have viewed the error in the *Begriffsschrift*'s view of the proposition as

---

[154] Cf. *PT*, 4.11: "A proposition asserts the existence of the situation whose possibility it portrays [*darstellt*]" (translation mine).

arising from the illicit attempt to externalize and separately express these two internal (hence inseparable) aspects of the proposition. The *Annahme* is treated as the notational embodiment of the "showing" aspect of the proposition (picking out a situation while saying nothing about it), while the assertion sign is treated as embodying the proposition's "truth-claiming" or "saying" aspect (saying of the possible situation thus picked out that it actually obtains). I have wanted to suggest that Wittgenstein's critique of the assertion sign is best seen as part of an attack on the coherence of such a conception of the proposition.

## [12] FINAL CONSIDERATIONS

I want to turn finally to the last of our original six theses: "(3) some propositions assert their own truth." It is far from clear why Wittgenstein would have taken this thesis to be a component of any of Frege's views on assertion. To be sure, he would have regarded Frege as committed in *Grundgesetze* to the view that every proposition (logically) asserts *of a truth-value* that it is true, but this is not yet the view that any proposition asserts truth of *itself*. It would therefore seem that (3) cannot, after all, be part of the view Wittgenstein attributes to Frege. But what, then, is the point of Wittgenstein's denial of (3) at 4.442?

In my view we should read Wittgenstein as denying a precondition of any view that would try to make sense of a notion of distinctively *logical* assertion. The thought is that any such notion must combine two fundamentally incompatible ideas. On the one hand, in order to be a feature of *propositions*, logical assertion would need to govern the entire proposition. On the other, in order to be more than merely *psychological*, the feature of being asserted would have to be an intrinsic part of the proposition. The first thought steers us toward regarding "logical assertion" as something lying outside the proposition, for example, some merely psychological attitude one may hold towards it; while the second makes us think of it as an *element* of the proposition and, as such, capable of governing only its remaining parts. To avoid these conceptions while retaining the features wished for in a notion of truly *logical* assertion, one would need to invoke the idea of self-reference. The proposition would have to be conceived of as containing the thought of its own promulgation. But this is precisely the idea to which 4.442 takes exception: "A proposition cannot possibly say of itself that it is true."[155] Thus our only strategy for making sense of the notion of distinctively *logical* assertion is blocked. "Assertion," as Wittgenstein remarks in the *Notes on Logic*, "is merely psychological."[156]

In the end, then, the thought that a proposition cannot assert its own truth is best seen not as a direct criticism of any view that Frege or Russell actually hold, but as the denial of a crucial presupposition of the coherence of the notion of logical assertion.

---

[155] Unfortunately, it would lead us too far afield to investigate the grounds for this statement, but the point is connected with 3.332.
[156] *Notebooks*, p.95.

# CHAPTER 3

# The Proposition as a Picture of Reality

## INTRODUCTION

The aim of the *Tractatus*'s picture theory, broadly stated, is to make plausible that propositions are *representational* in nature, and that they are representational in the manner not of stand-ins or proxies, but in the manner of pictures. There are two relatively straightforward aspects to this claim, which Wittgenstein outlines in his discussion of pictures in the 2s. The first is captured by Wittgenstein's remark that "A picture agrees with reality or not; it is right or wrong, true or false" (2.21). To say that a proposition is a picture is to say that it is intrinsic to a proposition that it gets things right or wrong, agrees or fails to agree with reality, presents reality truly or falsely. For Wittgenstein, this is the *only* way a proposition can be true or false: "A proposition can be true or false only in virtue of being a picture of reality" (4.06). For him truth and falsehood are bound up with successful and unsuccessful representation: "The agreement or disagreement of [the picture's] sense with reality constitutes its truth or falsity" (2.222). This view contrasts with the position of, for example, Russell's *Principles*, according to which truth and falsity are two simple, indefinable properties that hold of a special class of complexes (those which have specifically *propositional* unity)[157]. Russell agrees

---

[157] That Russell views propositions as complexes of a special kind is evident from the following remark in "The Nature of Truth" of 1905:

> Propositions are complexes of a certain kind, for some complexes are not propositions—for example, "the cow with the crumpled

*Continued on next page*

with Wittgenstein in taking all propositions to be true or false, but because, at this stage,[158] he does not take truth to amount to agreement with reality, and falsehood to lack of agreement, his view leaves it seeming like an accident that every proposition is true or false. As Wittgenstein puts the point:

> One could...believe that the words "true" and "false" signify two properties among other properties, and then it would appear as a remarkable fact that every proposition possesses one of these properties. This now by no means appears self-evident,[159] no more than the proposition "All roses are either yellow or red" would sound even if it were true. (6.*111*)

In other words, by treating truth and falsity as two properties among others, Russell leaves it looking intelligible that propositions should fail to have either property. It then seems that if it should turn out that every proposition has one or other of these properties, that would be no more than a happy accident.

Wittgenstein's assumption that truth consists in agreement or disagreement with reality, of course, looks worryingly close to a correspondence theory of truth. The difference, however, is that Wittgenstein will make no attempt to cash the notion of "agreement" in other terms. The view is proffered only as a foil to Russell and Moore (and Frege), not as an explanatory theory in its own right. That is to say, talk of "agreement" and "disagreement" gestures at what is wrong with the Russell-Moore view. It does not try to break out of the circle of inter-defined notions in terms of which the picture theory is developed.

---

horn"Charles I's execution", etc. Propositions are distinguished, as a rule, in language, by the presence of a verb; and verbs seem to be used to express just that particular kind of complexity which propositions have and other complexes do not have. But I do not know how to describe this kind of complexity. (*CP Vol. IV*, p. 503)

[158] Later, of course, when he had changed his mind about the bearers of truth and falsity—taking them to be judgements or beliefs rather than propositions—Russell came to adopt a version of the correspondence theory of truth. Russell's change of mind begins with some indecisive remarks in his 1906 paper "On the Nature of Truth" *Proceedings in the Aristotelian Society*, New Series Vol. 7, 1906-7. It is fully evident in his 1910 essay "On the Nature of Truth and Falsehood" *PE*, pp. 147–59, and in *POP*, p. 70.

[159] Wittgenstein is here helping himself for the sake of argument to (what he takes to be) Russell's view that there is a close link between logical truth and self-evidence.

The second more or less straightforward aspect to Wittgenstein's calling a proposition a "picture" is the idea that what the proposition represents is unchanged by its success or failure in representing the world. He says: "The picture represents what it represents, independently of its truth or falsehood..." (2.22). Since a proposition's identity is bound up with its representing what it does, this is tantamount to saying that a proposition is what it is independently of its particular truth value. Though, of course, that is not to say that it could be what it is independently of having one or other truth value.[160] On the contrary, the proposition's feature of being a representation—hence of being a proposition at all—is bound up with its success or failure in representing the world.[161]

Wittgenstein's stated ground for holding a proposition to be a picture is, however, distinct from either of these. It is contained in the following remark:

> The proposition is a picture of reality, for I know the state of affairs presented by it, if I understand the proposition. And I understand the proposition, without its sense having been explained to me. (4.021)

I shall argue in this chapter that this remark contains the heart of the picture theory: what is central to calling a proposition "a picture of reality" is that I can understand a proposition (hence know the situation it represents) without its sense having been explained to me. A proposition contains its own resources for putting me in touch with the situation it represents.[162] As Wittgenstein puts the point in the *Notebooks*:

> The proposition presents a situation as it were off its own bat (*auf eigene Faust*). (5th November 1914) (*Notebooks*, p. 26)

---

[160] My talk of "truth values" here is intended only as an abbreviated way of speaking of the proposition being true or false, I don't mean to suggest that Wittgenstein is operating with anything like Frege's notion of a truth value.

[161] Wittgenstein states the point most clearly in the *Moore Notes*. He says: "To have meaning *means* to be true or false: the being true or false actually constitutes the relation of the proposition to reality, which we mean by saying that it has meaning (*Sinn*)." (*Notebooks*, p. 113.)

[162] Compare Wittgenstein's attitude toward tautologies: they contain their own resources for showing themselves to be tautologies, for showing, that is to say, that they say–or represent–nothing.

The idea that this point is particularly central to the picture theory receives further support from a careful reading of 4.02, a proposition whose first word—'this'— can be seen—with some detective
work—to have as its intended reference 4.01, rather than the
proposition which immediately precedes it in the *Tractatus*—
4.016. (The detailed considerations leading to this conclusion are
set out in the Appendix.) It turns out, therefore, that the *Tractatus*
*ought* to run:[163]

> 4.01 The proposition is a picture of reality. The proposition
> is a model of reality as we imagine it.
>
> 4.02 This we see from the fact that we understand the sense
> of the propositional sign, without having had it explained to
> us.

Again, what alerts us to the pictorial character of the proposition
is what has come to be called "the creative aspect of language
use."[164] We can frame in language propositions we have never
encountered before and come to know what they say, without having this pointed out to us in every case. The reason we can do so
is that, knowing the meanings of the words, we can work out the
proposition's sense from the way the words are put together in the
propositional sign:

> A proposition must communicate a new sense with old
> words. (4.03)

In this chapter I want to think through how this insight about
what we should today call "compositionality" helps to inform the
central conceptions of the picture theory. From this starting point
I will work towards a reading of Wittgenstein's remarks that aims
to make it plausible that the picture theory might have been operating as Wittgenstein's way of solving, or dissolving, the problem
of the unity of the proposition. I want to begin, however, by trying
to motivate Wittgenstein's position by discussing a problem that
arises for Russell's way of thinking about language.

---

[163] We cannot glean this from the numbering system since 4.02 is the second comment on 4.0, not a comment on 4.01.
[164] The thought that language has such an aspect is a very early one, stem-
ming from the *1913 Notes on Logic*: "We must be able to understand
propositions which we have never heard before." (*Notebooks*, p. 98)

## [2] RUSSELL

In the *Principles* Russell does not concern himself with questions of how a sentence comes to express the proposition it expresses. At this stage of his thinking he sees language as "transparent" in the sense that it perfectly, or near perfectly, recapitulates the structure of the thoughts it expresses. Because of this transparency, Russell believes he can set aside language and theorize directly about the propositions it expresses.[165] But, ironically, Russell's implicit views about language—the views that motivate his lack of interest in it—land him in serious trouble on this very point of creativity. On Russell's view it is quite unclear how one can know which proposition is expressed by a novel sentence (i.e. one we have never heard before and so one whose sense we have never had explained to us).

Take the sentence "Desdemona loves Othello." If language is transparent in the way Russell suggests then when we are presented with this sentence we will apprehend the propositional constituents, Desdemona, *loving* and Othello. But how will we apprehend their manner of combination? On Russell's account we can get as far as apprehending that the elements are combined in the manner appropriate to propositional complexes, for this is something that Russell takes to be indicated by the presence of the *linguistic* verb. In "The Nature of Truth" he writes:

> Propositions are distinguished, as a rule, in language, by the presence of the verb; and verbs seem to be used to express just that particular kind of complexity which propositions have and other complexes do not have. (op. cit., p. 503).

But how do we know just from the sentence that the elements are to be combined in the manner characteristic of the proposition that Desdemona loves Othello rather than in the manner characteristic of the proposition that Othello loves Desdemona? We should like to say that the mode of composition of the sentence mirrors the mode of composition of the proposition. But one encounters difficulties in trying to cash this thought out. It cannot mean that the elements of the proposition are combined in the proposition *exactly* as they are combined in the sentence, for the elements of the sentence stand in spatial relations to one another and, whatever the relations of the elements

---

[165] I owe the idea that Russell saw language as transparent in this way to Peter Hylton. See Hylton, op. cit., p. 171.

in the proposition might be, they are not spatial. So Russell's view leaves it looking as though we should need to be told the sense of each sentence before we can understand it.

Wittgenstein offers an account shows how this conclusion may be avoided. His account seeks to close the gap between a sentence and the proposition it expresses. It suggests that we can have no conception of a proposition independently of the language by means of which it is expressed. For Wittgenstein, the proposition just *is* the propositional sign in its projective relation to the world (3.12).

## [3] THE PICTURE THEORY

What is it for a proposition to be a "picture of reality"?[166] We know propositions are facts (2.141). We also know that a picture is a fact (2.141) and that picturing is supposed to involve a sharing of a pictorial form (*Form der Abbildung*) between distinct facts (2.17), where:

> Pictorial form is the possibility that things are related to one another in *the same way* as the elements of the picture. (2.151) (My emphasis)

We can use these points to home in on the idea of a picture of reality. After saying that a picture is a fact, Wittgenstein continues:

> That the elements of the picture are combined with one another in a definite way represents that the things are so combined. (2.15)

So, for example, in a spatial picture (by which I mean a picture whose pictorial form is spatiality) the fact that certain elements stand in a particular spatial relationship is used to represent the fact that certain other elements stand in the very same spatial relationship. For example, the model truck's being to the right of the motorcycle represents the actual truck's having been so related to the actual motorcycle during the accident. Similarly, a picture whose pictorial form is color—or coloredness (*Färbigkeit*) (2.0251)—uses the very colors of elements in the picturing fact to represent that the objects for which they go proxy stand so char-

---

[166] This section is heavily indebted to Peter Sullivan's "A Version of the Picture Theory," in W. Vossenkuhl, ed., *Wittgenstein: Tractatus* (Akademie Verlag, 1997).

acterized in the reality depicted. For example, the blueness of the "sky" in the child's painting represents the real sky as so colored. By thus incorporating certain features of the reality it represents, a spatial or colored picture achieves a peculiar intimacy with its object. As Wittgenstein puts it: "Thus the picture is linked with reality; it reaches up to it" (2.1511).

But we could represent these same facts without relying on shared features or relations between objects in the picturing fact and objects in what is pictured. For the "naturalistic" pictures we have so far considered are not the only pictures there are. We could, for example, color-code a child's painting so that, for example, the redness of the paper is supposed to represent the blueness of the sky, and we would still have a representation of a blue sky. Colored pictures can successfully depict what they do depict without having colored pictorial form. In such a case the colors in the picture will be significant, but their playing a role in representing what they do represent will not depend on their being identical with features of the sentence depicted. Colored form is not essential to picturing. What every picture must have, however, to be a picture at all is logical form:

> What any picture, of whatever form, must have in common
> with reality in order to be able to represent it at all—rightly
> or falsely— is logical form,[167] that is, the form of reality. (2.18)

Logical form, then, is the least determinate pictorial form. It is what any picture must share with reality if representation is to take place at all.

We are not told directly what logical form is. Wittgenstein explains the notion by presenting it as the limit of a process of abstraction from the material aspects of picturing form. An architect's three-dimensional model might use terracotta colored cardboard to represent the hue of the brickwork in the planned building; or it might use a color-coding scheme. In the former case, the fact that pieces of card are terracotta colored will represent the fact that bricks are so colored. In the latter case, color will be represented, but its representation will not involve a sharing of color between elements of the model and elements of reality: the picture

---

[167] Notice Wittgenstein's very special use of the term "logical form." For Wittgenstein it is only pictures that have logical form in this sense. So a tautology, for example, will not have a logical form, though it will have the general form of the proposition.

(or model) will have color but lack colored pictorial form. But because the three-dimensional configuration of the elements will involve the sharing of spatial relations between model and reality, the model will still have spatial pictorial form. We can imagine abstracting from the spatial features of the representation, too, for we can imagine representing spatial relations by means of a complex system of temporal relations. A particular pitch might be given the task of expressing the direction North; and its duration in seconds, the length in meters proceeding in that direction from a particular spot. The two other spatial dimensions might be represented by two other pitches, so that a three-note "chord" played on a particular instrument specifies a point in a three-dimensional co-ordinate system. We could go on to use the dimension of timbre to represent a range of instructions on how the co-ordinate system is to be filled in. If a chord is played on a piano, we are to put a brick in the place indicated by its three pitches; if by the harp, the space is to be left blank. If a trumpet sounds simultaneously, the brick is to have North–South orientation in the plane; if not, East–West; etc. By playing our chords successively we will be able to give a complete representation of the brick-work of the building.

Now we will have abstracted from the spatiality of the model. Spatial representations will no longer be represented by being shared between the picture and what it depicts. And our picture will therefore lack spatial pictorial form. Nor will the sound-picture be a temporal picture, for although the chords will be ordered in time, temporal relations and properties will not be shared between the picture and the reality it depicts. What we have described, rather, will be merely a *logical* picture of a state of affairs.

Our cacophony will not be a blend of notes, for it will have a definite structure, albeit one that in practice will be hard to discern. Each note played on each instrument will make a distinctive contribution to the outcome, a contribution it could also have made to the depiction of a different arrangement of bricks. Similarly, for Wittgenstein the proposition is not a *blend* or *mixture* of words (3.141). It is "articulate" in the sense that it says what it does say by means of distinct words, each of which makes its own contribution to what is said.[168]

---

[168] Wittgenstein's point *really* is that it's not a *blend* (*not* that it's not an

*Continued on next page*

The notion of a logical picture inherits from spatial pictures some of the transparency of the idea of picturing, but simultaneously dispenses with the limitations of the models which—so to speak—give the idea of picturing its color. We are left with the bare idea of a model—a model of reality. What the abstract idea of a logical picture retains is the notion that a *range* of facts about certain items can be used to represent a *range* of situations, and in such a way that we can grasp the significance of new facts in the range on the basis of our understanding of members of the range whose significance is already known. The logical form of the picture is a matter of the logical multiplicity of the system of representation.

It should be clear from these reflections that picturing is not merely the holding of an isomorphism between facts. I may establish a convention that the presence of a top hat on the head of the statue of Lincoln in the Lincoln Memorial is to mean that Clinton is in the White House. In such a case I will be using one fact of the form 'xRy' to express another fact of this form. But the one fact will not yet be a *picture* of the other. Rather, the fact that a certain hat is on the head of Lincoln will merely go proxy for the proposition that Clinton is in the White House. What is missing is what Wittgenstein calls *logical articulation*:

> The proposition is a picture of a state of affairs, only in so far
> as it is logically articulated. (4.032)

The articulation of a fact becomes a *logical* articulation when the components of the fact are given independent meanings that admit of recombination to yield *new* pictures:

> It is essential to a proposition that it can communicate a new
> sense to us. (4.027)[169]

---

unordered jumble or collection). He writes to Ogden: "The main stress does NOT lie on the point that the proposition isn't a disordered higgledy[-]piggledy sort of combination of words, but merely on the point that it is no MIXTURE at all but a STRUCTURE." (*LO*, p. 24).

[169] It should be mentioned that Wittgenstein has not argued for this claim. Compositionality reveals that *some* propositions can communicate new senses, but this is a stronger claim, whose justification is unclear. It may be that Wittgenstein is operating with the tacit assumption that there must be a *uniform* explanation of the proposition, so if some are logically articulated, all must be.

If one fact is to *picture* another, I will have to set up a convention governing the significance of the occurrence of a range of facts involving its elements. I might stipulate, for example, that the fact that the hat in question is on a statue designed by Daniel Chester French is to say that Clinton is in the city containing the statue. Now we no longer have a fact which serves as a stand-in for a proposition. And that we do not is shown by the fact that when I come across a new fact about this hat which I have not encountered before, and whose significance has not yet been explained to me—say, the fact that it is on the statue of John Harvard in Harvard Yard—I will be able to work out its significance from my knowledge of the general significance of facts of this form. It is this feature that makes a fact a picture of reality, hence a proposition.

## [4] PROPOSITIONAL CONSTITUENTS

Until now I have been emphasizing the sharing of logical form between proposition and fact, but of course the other side of the story is that some elements in the proposition *go proxy* for elements in the state of affairs represented. Wittgenstein sees this as an essential feature making representation possible. As he puts it in the *Notebooks*:

> The possibility of the proposition is, of course, founded on the principle of signs as GOING PROXY for objects. (*Notebooks*, p. 37)

The simple signs in an elementary proposition go proxy for objects in the state of affairs it represents. "In the state of affairs," says Wittgenstein, "objects hang in one another like the links of a chain"(2.03). The meaning of this remark is spelled out in Wittgenstein's explanation of it to Ogden:

> The meaning is *that there isn't anything third* that connects the links but that the links *themselves* make connexion with one another. (*Letters*, p. 23)

What goes for the state of affairs also goes for the elementary proposition by which it is depicted. Elementary propositions "consist of names in immediate combination" (4.221 cf. 5.55). So there is nothing beyond the names to link them together.

This raises the question how we are to understand apparent relational expressions, such as the 'R' in the propositional sign 'aRb'. Are we to think of them as names or as signifying in some other way? What is clear is that we cannot think of 'R' as a name for a relation. For if we do—if we think of it as a genuine name and so as going proxy for a relation—we will need to think of the relation it stands for as an item which—rather like Russell's verb of the proposition—serves to unite the elements of the complex into a whole. Otherwise we shall only have a list of names, not a proposition. But this is clearly ruled out by the explanation of 2.03 to Ogden.

I think the way out of these difficulties is to follow a line of thought suggested by Anscombe and further developed by Thomas Ricketts.[170] We should treat what we naively think of as the propositional constituent expressed by a relational expression as an aspect of the form of the proposition, that is to say, as something properly expressed by the *way* in which the names are combined in the propositional sign.

To make any sense of this idea we would need to conceive of a propositional sign as something with both fact-like and thing-like aspects—a "complex" in Russell and Wittgenstein's terminology. (I believe this way of viewing the propositional sign is warranted by Wittgenstein's confessed failure to distinguish adequately in the *Tractatus* between complex and fact.[171]) Consider the propositional sign "a loves b" thought of as a complex of the expressions "a", "loves," and "b". In this sign we can perceive a number of significant elements. We can perceive the names "a" and "b", but also the way in which these names are combined. We can perceive this mode of combination if we can appreciate that *other* names might have been combined in precisely this way. We can learn the significance of the names by learning which objects they go proxy for. We learn the significance of their manner of

---

[170] See Anscombe op. cit., pp. 89 ff , and Thomas Ricketts's "Pictures, logic, and the limits of sense in Wittgenstein's *Tractatus*," in *The Cambridge Companion to Wittgenstein*, Hans Sluga and David Stern, eds. (Cambridge: Cambridge University Press, 1996), pp. 59–99.

[171] In the appendix to the *Philosophical Grammar*, entitled "Complex and Fact" of 1931 Wittgenstein writes: "The fact that these links [of a chain] are so concatenated, isn't '*composed*' of anything at all." *PG*, p. 201. Given the reference to a "chain" at 2.03 and given that the *Tractatus* explains an elementary proposition both as a concatenation of names *and* as a fact—it is a propositional sign (or symbolizing fact) in its projective relation to the world, this remark is very plausibly directed against the Tractarian conception of an atomic fact.

combination, however, in a quite different way, namely by means of a clause stating the significance of a range of facts (or complexes)[172] which combine elements in precisely that way. For example, the significance of the way in which the names "a" and "b" are combined in the complex/propositional sign "a loves b" is explained by the following clause:

(1)$\forall$x $\forall$y (that a token of x stands immediately to the left of a token of 'loves' which stands immediately to the left of a token of y says that what x names loves what y names).[173]

In (1) the variables range over a domain of (referring)[174] names.

It is thus *relations* between signs in the propositional sign that express relations between objects in the fact depicted.[175] I take this idea to be implicit in Wittgenstein's remark at 3.1432: "*That 'a' stands in a certain relation to 'b' says that* aRb." Assuming 'Mary' and 'Jim' refer, an instance of (1) would be:

(2)  that a token of 'Mary' stands immediately to the left of a token of 'loves' which stands immediately to the left of a token of 'Jim' says that what 'Mary' names loves what 'Jim' names.[176]

Understanding the proposition 'Mary loves Jim' therefore requires seeing the sentence 'Mary loves Jim' as 'tokening' (in the sense of chapter I[177]) a fact or complex of the form:

---

[172] It is here that we need this qualification, because we cannot strictly make sense of the way in which objects are combined in a fact, but only in a thing.

[173] We have a semantics expressed in pseudo-propositions; strictly speaking: "Facts cannot be *named*" (*Notebooks* p. 107).

[174] The qualification "referring" would, of course, be unnecessary if we were dealing with the symbols that the *Tractatus* regards as genuine names.

[175] Richard Heck observes that this view provides a satisfying unification of the sense in which a relation and the symbol for a relation may be thought of as "unsaturated." For Frege a relational expression is not unsaturated in the same sense as its reference, for a relational expression is an *object*. For Wittgenstein, by contrast, because the symbol for a relation is a relation, symbol and sign are unsaturated in precisely the same sense. (Of course, whether we can ultimately make sense of this talk of "saturation" and "unsaturation" is a separate question.)

[176] We can bring out the fact that (2) conforms to the pattern of 3.1432 if, following a suggestion of Thomas Ricketts, we think of 'Mary' as standing in the relation of LOVES-leftflanking to 'John'. See Ricketts, "Pictures," p. 71 ff.

[177] See chapter I, section 2.

(3) that a token of ∝ stands immediately to the left of a token 'loves' which stands immediately to the left of a token of β

where 'α' and 'β' are schematic letters, replaceable by names of names.

So if we were asked to identify the meaning-bearing elements in the proposition expressed by the sentence 'Mary loves Jim', we should have to say that they are the names 'Jim' and 'Mary' and the particular manner in which they are combined.

Notice that on this view of the meaning-bearing elements of the proposition, I cannot be in the position I seemed to be able to be in on the Russellian account. I cannot be in the position of knowing what the meaning-bearing elements of the propositional sign are, and *of knowing their meanings*, while not appreciating the significance of their being so combined. For the way in which the names are combined just is one of the meaning-bearing elements of the proposition. My knowing the meaning of the fact that a token of 'loves' stands between tokens of two names x and y, just consists in my knowing that when this is so this fact signifies that what x names loves what y names. If I know this, and if I know the meanings of the names 'Mary' and 'Jim', I cannot fail to know the significance of the fact that these names stand combined in the way they do in the sentence (or Inscription) 'Mary loves Jim'. And to know the significance of this fact is just to understand the proposition that Mary loves Jim.

## [5] THE UNITY OF THE PROPOSITION

This view offers the materials for a solution to—or, more correctly, a dissolution of—the problem of the unity of the proposition. It also provides a plausible way of motivating Wittgenstein's view of nonsense. The problem of the unity of the proposition is dissolved once we arrive at the correct view of the proposition's meaning-bearing elements. The problem arises only if we can make sense of the idea of an inappropriate combination of meaningful parts. For only then can we ask what it is that holds the parts together in an appropriate combination.

But what might seem to be an inappropriate combination of meaningful signs—'Socrates Plato', for example—will turn out to be a string that contains certain signs that fail to have a meaning.

The example is taken from a passage in the *Moore Notes*, where Wittgenstein makes clear that at the time of writing he had already arrived at the conception of nonsense one finds in the *Tractatus*. He says:

> The reason why, e.g. it seems as if "Plato Socrates" might have a meaning, while "Abracadabra Socrates" will never be suspected to have one, is because we know that "Plato" has one, and do not observe that in order that the whole phrase should have one, what is necessary is not *that* "Plato" should have one, but that the fact that "Plato" *is to the left of a name* should. (*Notebooks*, p. 116).

Compare the remark from *Tractatus* 5.4733:

> Frege says: Every legitimately constructed proposition must have a sense; and I say: Every possible proposition is legitimately constructed, and if it has no sense this can only be because we have given no meaning to some of its constituent parts.
>
> (Even if we believe that we have done so.)
>
> Thus "Socrates is identical" says nothing, because we have given *no* meaning to the word "identical" as *adjective*....

The reason "Plato Socrates" might *seem* to have a meaning is that both 'Plato' and 'Socrates' have a meaning in the language (which is to say that there are some meaningful sentences in which these expressions do function as names). Accordingly, we fail to treat "Plato Socrates" as a sentence containing a nonsense word. But our failure to do so is attributable to an illusion arising from an incorrect view of the meaning-bearing elements of a sentence; they are not all words; rather, some of them are modes of combination of words.

To appreciate this point, let us consider how the illusion may be resisted by keeping in mind the view of the meaning-bearing elements of a sentence we have just outlined when trying to make sense of the string 'Plato Socrates'. We might begin by supposing that 'Socrates' functions in the sentence as a name. If we additionally suppose that 'Plato' is a syntactically integral string,[178] this will

---

[178] We are not forced to make this assumption, but other assumptions we might make—for example, that 'P' is a name and the fact that 'P' and "Socrates" flank 'lato' in that order is a significant fact—will lead to a conclusion similar to the one we reach by pursing the present assumption.

commit us to supposing that the fact that 'Plato' occurs to the left of a name is a meaning-bearing element. But this is not one that has been given significance in the language of which we take 'Plato Socrates' to be a sentence. But if not, then 'Plato' is not functioning as an adjective, and that means, in turn, that 'Socrates' is not, *after all*, functioning as a name.[179] So we have a string of letters, or an Inscription in the sense of chapter I, but this Inscription does not token any facts that could serve as propositional signs.

So the feared possibility of an inappropriate combination of meaningful signs in the end turns out not to be a genuine possibility, but only the appearance of one. It follows that we cannot get ourselves into a position where the question about the unity of the proposition can arise, a position where the presuppositions of the question: "what binds these meaning-bearing elements together into a proposition?" are satisfied. (Hence a position where we might feel compelled to fish around for some privileged element to do the work of binding the other elements into a proposition: a 'verb' in the linguistic sense of Russell's 1904-5 writings.) For the question only makes sense against the background of a coherent alternative to be excluded.

It is tempting to try to put this point by saying: If we don't get sense, we don't get the meaning-bearing elements either; but that is not quite right. We saw (in chapter I) that Wittgenstein thinks of tautologies and contradictions as containing meaning-bearing elements whose combination into a whole does not result in sense. The proper way to put the point is by saying that we cannot think of nonsense as resulting from the inappropriate combination of meaningful parts.[180] If we have nonsense, it is not because we have meaning-bearing elements that fail to gel, but because we fail to find any meaning-bearing elements in the first place.

It is in this way—by getting the right view of the proposition— that we motivate Wittgenstein's view of nonsense. This point is important, for it avoids certain problems faced by another way of trying to motivate the view.

---

[179] Here, I am relying on the context principle as interpreted by Diamond and Goldfarb. See Diamond, *The Realistic Spirit*, ch. 6 and Goldfarb, "Metaphysics and Nonsense."
[180] This point is made forcefully in Diamond, loc. cit.
[181] See Diamond, *The Realistic Spirit*, ch. 3.

In her article "What Nonsense Might Be,"[181] Cora Diamond contrasts Wittgenstein's view of nonsense with what she alleges to be[182] the natural view of nonsense. She characterizes the natural view as the view that a nonsense sentence such as "Caesar is a prime number" owes its meaninglessness to what its component words mean: they have meanings that somehow fail to cohere to produce sense.[183] Wittgenstein's view is that, as she puts it: "there is no kind of nonsense which is nonsense on account of what the terms composing it mean."[184] And the following consideration is meant to tell against the natural view and in favour of Wittgenstein's:

> The idea that the sentence is nonsense because of the categories of the expressions illegitimately combined in it is implicitly the idea of their forming a sentence which *does* say something—which the holder of the natural view regards as an impossibility and which he denies is really sayable at all: this is the incoherence of the natural view as seen from the Frege-Wittgenstein position.[185]

Diamond's idea is that those who see nonsense as resulting from the attempt to combine meaningful expressions in a way that is ruled out by their meanings are tacitly committed to regarding a sentence as nonsense on the grounds that it says something which turns out to be an impossibility. They are committed to saying, for example, that 'Socrates is identical', depicts the object Socrates as characterized by a relation in the manner in which he might be

---

[182] I'm doubtful that Jabberwocky sentences, for example, would "naturally" be thought of in this way, rather than in Wittgenstein's way. On the other hand, this is plausibly how people would regard Chomsky's "Colorless green ideas sleep furiously".

[183] A proponent of the "natural view," with whose writings Wittgenstein's could have been acquainted—though I know of no positive evidence that at this stage he was—is Edmund Husserl. In § 14 of the fourth investigation of his *Logische Untersuchungen* (first published 1900–1901; second revised edition (Halle: Niemeyer, 1913–1920)) when discussing rules for the avoidance of nonsense (*Unsinn*) as opposed to illogicality (*Widersinn*), Husserl writes:

> The word 'nonsense'—let us stress it again—must be understood in its literal, strict sense. A heap of words like *King but or like and* cannot be understood as a unit: each word has sense in isolation, but the compound is without sense. (Translation my own)

I owe this point to Charles Parsons.

[184] Diamond, *The Realistic Spirit*, p. 106.

[185] Ibid., p. 105.

characterized by a property, so that a *clash* of meanings renders the whole nonsense. Diamond's criticism thus amounts to the charge that proponents of the natural view fail to take fully seriously the idea that the sentence is nonsense, for they see it as a coherent *depiction* of an impossible situation.

But the charge is not obviously a fair one. Perhaps *some* of those committed to the view that nonsense arises from the illegitimate combination of meaningful expressions have appealed to the idea of depicting the impossible, but it is not obvious that one who champions natural view need make this mistake. An alternative way of fleshing out the natural view might be to appeal to some variant of Chomsky-style "selection rules," which on some more modern treatments are taken to operate at the level of the semantics.[186] On this view, 'The table drinks the square root of three' would fail to say anything because: a) one of the selectional features of the word 'drinks' is that it takes as complement a noun-phrase that is marked with the selectional feature 'concrete', while the complex numeral 'the square route of three' lacks (or is negatively marked for) this feature; and b) another of 'drinks''s selectional features is that it takes as subject a noun phrase that is positively marked for the feature "animate" while the noun phrase 'the table' is negatively marked for this feature. On this approach we explain the meaninglessness of the whole sentence by appeal to (aspects of) the meanings of the parts, but not by treating the sentence as depicting the referents as fitting together in an impossible way.

For all I know, this account may be false, but it is not on the face of it incoherent, and it certainly does not involve the schizophrenic attitude to the meaningfulness of the sentence that is supposed to characterize proponents of what Diamond calls the "natural view." There is no hint of talk here of what the sentence would *represent* if, *per impossibile*, it made sense.

One virtue I would claim for the interpretation I have suggested is that it avoids having to portray proponents of the natural view as espousing an obviously unattractive position, and so

---

[186] Noam Chomsky, *Aspects of the Theory of Syntax* (Cambridge Mass.: MIT Press, 1965), pp. 95–97. It is an open question in linguistics at which level such selection restrictions are supposed to operate. But, however they operate, they will be of help to the defender of the natural view so long as a word's selectional features can be thought of as part of its meaning (in a broad sense).

makes Wittgenstein's alternative seem all the more illuminating. Another virtue is that it is fully in the spirit of Wittgenstein's insistence that the problems he faces will be solved by getting the correct view of the proposition: "My *whole* task," he says in the *Notebooks*, "consists in explaining the nature of the proposition." (January, 22nd, 1915, *Notebooks*, p. 39).

# CHAPTER 4

# Deductive Inference and its Justification

## INTRODUCTION

The philosophical problem of the justification of deduction is not one problem but many. This is partly because there are many respects in which the practice of deduction might be thought to stand in need of justification, but partly also because there is more than one thing that might be taken to be the intended *object* of justification, more than one thing that we might mean by "deduction" in the present context. Before getting down to the main business of this chapter— namely, the issue of the *Tractatus*'s views on deduction and its justification— I want to spend a little time distinguishing some of these senses.

Sometimes we speak of a deduction as the act of making a judgement on the basis of a particular body of evidence. We might say, for example, that Sherlock Holmes deduced the time of the murder from the position of the stopped hands in the victim's shattered pocket watch. Upon being asked (1)[187] what justifies a particular deduction, in this sense of deduction, we will usually answer by citing some of the evidence upon which the agent drew in making the inference, and in citing this evidence we shall be presupposing that the agent was *justified*—at least by her lights—in drawing the inference. If we have this sense of "deduction" foremost in our minds, the question: "what *in general* justifies deduction?" is likely to strike us as puzzling, and to do so for the kinds of reason that J. L. Austin thought the question "what-is-the-

---

[187] I will number the various senses of the question as I come to them.

meaning-of a word" puzzling.[188] For the question seems to be asking us to cite a standard body of evidence upon which all deductions are based, and, of course, there is no such thing—no more than there is a standard meaning possessed by all words.

Nevertheless, from time to time philosophers have attempted to give meaning to a justificatory question posed at this level of generality. One such philosopher is the Tortoise in Lewis' Carroll's famous dialogue: "What the Tortoise said to Achilles." The Tortoise wants to know (2) what could *compel* him to draw the conclusion of a deductively valid argument, given that he has accepted the premises. The short answer—as Achilles spends the dialogue discovering—is that nothing at all *compels* one to draw the conclusion, for, as the Tortoise demonstrates, one can always resist. And this is surely what we should expect. For if I could *not* resist, then having judged that p, I would be compelled to go on and judge that p or q and thereby be *further* compelled to go on to judge that p or q or q and similarly compelled to infer every other member of this tiresome series. And that is plainly not the case. Nor is it true to say that I'm even rationally obliged to infer every consequence of what I believe, for as Gilbert Harman has emphasized,[189] it is equally a maxim of reason that one ought not to clutter one's mind with too many trivialities.

Of course, we can re-jig the Tortoise's question, so that it becomes a question about license rather than compulsion. And in so doing we will raise the more interesting question: (3) how are we to make sense of the license-issuing role of rules of inference? The moral of Carroll's dialogue, on this reading, is that we can not, on pain of an infinite regress, demand that everything appealed to in justifying a conclusion be treated as a *premise* of the argument. If inference is to be possible, some principles to which we appeal in drawing inferences must function otherwise than as premises. (I shall return to this point below.)

Another sense of the term "deduction," more common among philosophers than ordinary folk, is its use to refer to a whole deductive argument. We might say, for example, that Holmes carried out the following deduction. "If the butler didn't do it, then

---

[188] John L. Austin, *Philosophical Papers*, third edition, first published 1961 (Oxford: Oxford University Press), ch.3.
[189] Gilbert Harman, *Change in View: Principles of Reasoning* (Cambridge, Mass.: MIT Press, 1986), ch.2.

the gardener must have done, but the gardener didn't do it, so the butler must have done it after all." Were we to ask: (4) what justifies a *particular* deduction in this sense, we would most likely be asking someone to point to a valid pattern of reasoning of which the present concrete argument is an instance. (In the present case it would suffice to point out that we are reasoning by *modus tollens*.)

But another more perplexing question that could be asked about deductions in this sense is: (5) what in general *makes* the good ones, such as *modus tollens*, good? In asking this question we will be asking what relation the premises bear to the conclusion in virtue of which it is true to say that the argument is formally valid. One answer to this question is the Tarski-Quine answer: the relation in question is the relation of logical consequence—a relation which holds between premises and conclusion just in case the argument can be schematized by a schema which is valid in the sense of being true on every interpretation of its non-logical vocabulary. Of course, the question has now transformed itself into the question of the correct analysis of the intuitive notion of logical entailment. But, as we shall see, this kind of question can be precisely the question philosophers have meant to be asking when asking what *in general* justifies an inference or a deduction?

This last question is related to another that has figured prominently in the writings of Michael Dummett. As Dummett's work makes clear, it is at least conceivable that one's analysis of the notion of entailment might be one that failed to validate certain arguments that are intuitively valid. For if one's analysis appeals to the notion of *truth*, there will be a question of how this notion is to be understood. And if there are good reasons to suppose that truth must be understood, for example, intuitionistically, then certain forms of argument which in our innocence we take to be intuitively valid—such as double negation elimination—will turn out not to be valid after all. For this reason it may sometimes not be particular arguments that are directly in question when we ask after the justification of deduction, but rather whole patterns of argument. We may want to know: (6) which forms of reasoning are properly licensed by our conception of truth? Now this issue goes far beyond the scope of the present inquiry. But I mention it in order to show just how wide the range of issues covered by the question of the justification of deduction can be.

The final version of the question I want to mention is again one that has been emphasized by Michael Dummett. This is the question: (7) "how is deductive inference possible?" Dummett raises the following worry: If deductive inferences are to be useful, they must be informative; but if they are to be justified, then, in recognizing the truth of the premises, I must in some sense already have recognized whatever is necessary for recognizing the truth of the conclusion, but if so, then it is hard to see how deductive inferences can have any chance of *extending* our knowledge.[190] Some account seems to be owed of how deductive inference can be both warranted and useful.

With these various questions distinguished, I want to turn to Wittgenstein's discussion of inference in the *Tractatus*. Before examining Wittgenstein's answer I will first locate the question Wittgenstein is addressing and set it in its historical context. My broader purposes will be first, to ask whether Wittgenstein has anything to say about the notions of inference, entailment and deduction that might be of interest to contemporary philosophy, and secondly, to use Wittgenstein's discussion of these issues as a means of illustrating an important aspect of his philosophical method in the *Tractatus*. The main focus of the chapter will be on questions (5) and (7).

## [1] LAWS OF INFERENCE

What, then, does Wittgenstein actually say about the justification of deduction in the *Tractatus*? A key text is *Tractatus 5.132*:

> If *p* follows from *q*, I can make an inference from *q* to *p*; deduce *p* from *q*.
>
> The method of inference is to be gathered from the two propositions alone.
>
> Only they themselves can justify the inference.
>
> "Laws of inference"[191] [*Schlussgesetze*], which—as in Frege and Russell—are to justify the inferences, are senseless [*sinn-los*] and would be superfluous [*überflüssig*]. (5.132)
>
> (My translation)

---

[190] Michael Dummett, *The Logical Basis of Metaphysics* (Cambridge, Mass.: Harvard University Press, 1991), pp. 195 ff.

[191] The German contains quotation-marks which are missing from Ogden's translation.

Wittgenstein is clear about what in his view justifies a deductive inference, namely, nothing beyond the premise and conclusion of the argument, but it is much less obvious to which question this is supposed to be the answer. We know that Wittgenstein is presenting his view as an alternative to the views of Russell and Frege, so one avenue for progress will be to investigate the sense in which Frege and Russell might have taken their laws to be justificatory.

But first what did Wittgenstein *mean* by Russell's and Frege's "laws of inference"? The majority view among Wittgenstein commentators seems to be that in speaking of "laws of inference" Wittgenstein intends to be referring to the inference *rules* of an axiom system.[192] But an inspection of the relevant texts suggests that neither Frege nor Russell used the term "laws of inference" so narrowly. In discussing whether logical laws ought to be called axioms, Frege writes:

> Traditionally, what is called an axiom is a thought whose truth is certain without, however, being provable by a chain of logical inferences. The laws of logic, too, are of this nature. Some people may nevertheless be inclined to refrain from ascribing the name 'axiom' to these *general laws of inference* [*allgemeinen Gesetze alles Schließens*]...(Italics my own.)[193]

Here, clearly, Frege is treating the expression "*general laws of inference*" as a variant upon "laws of logic."

Russell's understanding of the phrase "laws of inference" can be gleaned from a passage in the paper "Necessity and Possibility," which he read to the Oxford Philosophical Society in 1905. He writes:

> There are certain general propositions, which we may enumerate as the laws of deduction: such are "if not-$p$ is false, then $p$ is true", "if $p$ implies not-$q$, then $q$ implies not-p" [and] "if $p$ implies $q$ and $q$ implies $r$, then $p$ implies r"; in all we need about ten such principles... (*CP Vol. IV*, p. 515)

---

[192] See, for example: Gordon Baker, *Wittgenstein, Frege and the Vienna Circle* (Oxford: Blackwell, 1988), p. 130; Anthony Kenny, *Wittgenstein*, first published 1973 (Harmondsworth: Penguin Books Ltd.), p. 98; H. O. Mounce, *Wittgenstein's Tractatus* (Oxford, Blackwell, 1981), p. 46.

[193] "Foundations of Geometry: First Series," *Collected Papers*, p. 319.

(By the way, a point that it will be important to remember throughout this chapter is that usually—though not always—Russell uses the word "implies" to express the relation of *material* implication, rather than entailment.) Now, since Russell tells us in a footnote to § 13 of the *Principles* that "[he does] not distinguish between inference and deduction", it seems reasonable to assume that the expression "laws of *deduction*" figures in this passage merely as a stylistic variant upon "laws of *inference*." But if so, then, Russell, too, would appear to be taking "laws of inference" to include logical laws.[194]

So our question becomes: why would Wittgenstein have seen either Russell or Frege as holding logical laws to be implicated in the justification of deductive arguments? In his paper "Frege, the *Tractatus* and the Logocentric Predicament"[195] Thomas Ricketts offers two kinds of answer to this question, both of which are worth considering. Ricketts takes Wittgenstein's criticism as applying in one way to Russell and in another to Frege.

Wittgenstein's criticism of Russell, as Ricketts understands it, focuses on his (alleged) failure adequately to distinguish inference rules from logical laws.[196] As Ricketts sees the matter, this confusion is bound up with a mistaken view of the way in which (what we would recognize as) inference rules confer license on the inferences they govern. According to Ricketts, Russell sees these rules—which for Ricketts' Russell are not to be distinguished from the laws of logic—as conferring their license only by serving as *premises* in arguments. Accordingly, Ricketts presents Wittgenstein as seeking to expose the errors of such a view by means of a tacit appeal to Lewis Carroll's regress argument.

---

[194] The fact that *modus ponens* is listed as an *axiom* in the *Principles* may suggest that for Russell laws of deduction include both logical laws and inference rules. I know of no clear evidence to confirm this, but I should not be troubled if it were so, for my disagreement is only with those commentators who would understand "laws of inference" in such a way as to exclude the laws of logic.

[195] Thomas Ricketts, "Frege, the *Tractatus*, and the Logocentric Predicament," *Noûs* (1985), pp. 3–15.

[196] See Ricketts, op. cit., p. 7: "Unlike Russell, Frege is absolutely clear on the difference between logical laws and inference rules, as well as the need for both in his axiomatic formulation of logic."

Suppose, for example, that *modus ponens* is taken to function as a *premise*. Then the argument from p and if p then q, to the conclusion q, will actually have the form:

p

p⊃q

(p&p⊃q)⊃q

Therefore, q

Here *modus ponens* is supposed to have been formulated as a proposition rather than as a rule. However, in this role it will be powerless to license the inference to the conclusion q because the argument is now of a new form, one not covered by *modus ponens*. Nor may we remedy the situation by appealing to some new inference rule, because *its* incorporation as a premise will again alter the overall shape of the argument and so only serve to fuel the regress.

As Ricketts admits, this story cannot be the whole explanation of Wittgenstein's critique of laws of inference, for there is no reason to suppose that *Frege* was at all inclined to treat inference rules as axioms. But, in my view, it is doubtful that this even captures Wittgenstein's criticism as it applies to Russell, for there is little reason to suppose that Russell collapsed the distinction between inference rules and logical laws in the way that Ricketts suggests.

The difficulty for Ricketts's reading is that Russell himself goes to great lengths to warn against precisely the error Ricketts attributes to him. In section 45 of the *Principles* Russell remarks: "In a particular inference the rule according to which the inference proceeds is *not* required as a premise." He then goes on to rehearse a Lewis Carroll-style argument in order to show that we should not, on pain of infinite regress, demand that the rule of universal instantiation be incorporated into arguments in the form of a *premise* which, in the context of *modus ponens*, would purport to license the relevant transition from a logical law to an instance.[197]

---

[197] Namely, the premise: "(a)(b)[(p)(q)(p&(p⊃q)⊃q)⊃a&(a⊃b)⊃b]".

Instead, Russell says that the rule according to which the inference proceeds represents what he terms "a respect in which the formalism breaks down." Russell concludes that inference rules are to
be accorded the status of informal principles that are employed in
making inferences but not incorporated as lines in proofs. [198]

Now it is true that Russell does *state* inference rules along with
logical laws in his list of "indemonstrable axioms" in section 18 of
the *Principles*, but this doesn't necessarily indicate that he was confused about the distinction between axioms and inference rules, or
that he took the latter to function as premises in arguments. The
*most* it shows, in my view, is that, for the purposes of identifying
the basic principles upon which mathematics rests, Russell does
not much *care* about the distinction between inference rules and
axioms. And it's easy to see why that should be so. On Russell's
treatment of them, both logical axioms and inference rules have
the status of primitive principles that neither need, nor admit of,
justification. So when identifying the fundamental grounds of
mathematics it makes sense to list the axioms and inference rules
together.

Since the *Principles of Mathematics* is one of the few works
of philosophy we know Wittgenstein to have read,[199] there is reason to think not only that *Russell* was not confused about the distinction between inference rules and axioms, but also that
Wittgenstein would have been very well aware of this fact. It seems
doubly unlikely, therefore, that Ricketts's account of Wittgenstein's
criticism of Russell can be the correct one.

Ricketts presents Wittgenstein's criticism of Frege as proceeding rather differently. His reading starts from the claim that for
Frege arguments whose premises and conclusion are non-logical
propositions may need to be[200] seen as mediated by laws of logic if
we are to make fully explicit the grounds on which the conclusion
rests. Consider, for example, the following argument:[201]

---

[198] Russell in fact overshoots his target, failing even to record universal
instantiation as an inference rule in the *Principia*. For Russell's later
acknowledgement of this oversight see *IMP*, p. 151, n. 1.
[199] The *Principles* is mentioned explicitly at 5.5351.
[200] I say "may need to be" because there will be some inferences, such as
an inference by *modus ponens*, that will not require such mediation.
[201] For an illuminating discussion of this conception of logic see Warren
Goldfarb, "Frege's Conception of Logic," forthcoming in J. Floyd and S.
Shieh, eds., *Futures Past: Reflections on the History and Nature of
Analytic Philosophy* (Cambridge, Mass.: Harvard University Press).
Ricketts gives a closely parallel account in "Pictures," p. 60.

i) All whales are mammals

ii) All mammals are vertebrates

Therefore, iii) All whales are vertebrates

According to Ricketts's Frege, i) and ii) do not exhaust the premises of this argument. Rather, there are additional suppressed premises of a logical nature. In order to prove the conclusion iii) we have to begin by deriving the following logical law from basic laws of logic:

iv) $(\forall F)(\forall G)(\forall H)[(\forall x)(Fx \supset Gx) \supset ((\forall x)(Gx \supset Hx) \supset (\forall x)(Fx \supset Hx))]$

We then proceed to instantiate the second-order variables in iv) to obtain:

v) $(\forall x)$(x is a whale $\supset$ x is a mammal) $\supset$ ($(\forall x)$(x is a mammal $\supset$ x is a vertebrate) $\supset$ $(\forall x)$(x is a whale $\supset$ x is a vertebrate)).

The conclusion, iii), then follows from i), ii) and v) by two applications of *modus ponens*.

Ricketts takes Wittgenstein to be opposing the idea that logical laws are needed to mediate inferences in this way. This view certainly provides a reasonable sense in which logical laws might be thought to justify inferences: they do so to the extent that they form part of the basis for the assertion of the conclusion. It is far from clear, however, that this could be the view that *Wittgenstein* is opposing at 5.123. For, if it were, we would expect him to claim that all this talk about "suppressed premises" is wrong, and that the true premises of the argument are just what they seem to be, namely, in our example, i) and ii). We would expect him to say that it is the truth of these premises, and these premises alone, that affords the justification for the conclusion. What Wittgenstein actually says, however, is rather different. He says that laws of inference are superfluous because the justification is afforded by premise *and conclusion* alone. Thus whatever *Wittgenstein* means by the "justification" of an inference, it must be something in which the conclusion itself can figure. Ricketts's account does not seem to meet this requirement, for it portrays the disagreement between Frege and Wittgenstein as one only about the correct premises for the inference. If Ricketts is right about the locus of the dispute then neither party to it should be appealing to the *conclusion* as part of the justification.

## [2] WITTGENSTEIN'S TRUE TARGET

What I have in mind as Wittgenstein's true target is an attempt to answer the fifth question that we discussed in our opening survey, namely, the question what kind of fact it is about a particular argument that makes it a valid argument. To suppose this to be the question at issue would certainly fit with Wittgenstein's citing the conclusion along with the premise as part of what in his view justifies the inference. But why should we think that Russell or Frege took laws of logic to be implicated in explaining what makes a particular deductive argument valid? How, for that matter, *would* one appeal to logical *laws* as part of the explanation of what makes an argument valid?

From one contemporary point of view the question almost answers itself. For Tarski and Quine, a logical law is a statement to the effect that a schema is valid, which is to say, true on every interpretation. So for these philosophers logical laws are naturally implicated in the explanation of what makes a particular argument intuitively valid. An argument is valid in the intuitive sense just in case it is schematized by a valid schema, and the statement that the schema is valid just *is* a logical law. However, from an historical perspective the question is far more puzzling. Neither Frege nor Russell had the contemporary notion of a schema available to them, and neither philosopher saw the laws of logic as metalinguistic statements about schemata. Rather, the logical laws for both philosophers are object-level generalizations in which none but logical vocabulary occurs. (Though I should mention that this is only a necessary, not a sufficient condition for being a logical law.)[202]

---

[202] As Richard Heck has pointed out, "$\exists x \forall F\ (x \neq \text{'}\epsilon F(\epsilon))$"—i.e. "there are objects distinct from value ranges"—is maximally general in the relevant sense, but does not seem to be a logical law. (If Frege did not see it as containing only logical vocabulary, then neither could he see axiom V as a logical law.)

Nonetheless, there are texts in Frege and Russell that might suggest the view Wittgenstein is criticizing. For example, in § 17 of *Grundlagen* Frege seems to treat the principles of mathematics—which for him are scarcely to be regarded as distinct from the principles of logic—as encoding inferential subroutines which can be used to justify particular arguments, but which must themselves be shown to follow from the basic laws of logic. But the view in question is most strongly suggested by some remarks of Russell's in the 1905 paper "Necessity and Possibility," from which I quoted earlier.

In this paper Russell is aiming to give an account of an intuitive notion which he terms "deducibility"—or once[203] "logical deducibility." Russell takes this notion to be an ordinary concept in need of precise definition. He takes himself to be trying to demarcate a class of material conditionals—or "implications" as he calls them—in which the consequent is intuitively felt to be a necessary consequence of the antecedent. He takes this to be the case when there is a "certain kind" of connection between antecedent and consequent. He writes:

> It is needful that the connection [of antecedent and consequent] should be of a certain kind in order that [the conditional] should be felt to be necessary. What this kind is, I shall shortly try to define: it may be loosely described as the kind which makes the consequent logically *deducible* from the antecedent. (*CP Vol IV*, p. 513)

Russell realizes that this feeling of necessity corresponds to a difference in the ground for our knowledge of the conditional in question. He writes:

> ...in the practice of inference, it is plain that something more than implication must be concerned. The reason that proofs are used at all is that we can sometimes perceive that *q* follows from *p*, when we should not otherwise know that *q* is true; while in other cases; "*p* implies *q*" is only to be inferred either from the falsehood of *p* or from the truth of *q*....What we require is a *logical* distinction between these two cases. (Ibid., p. 515)

---

[203] For example, *CP Vol. IV*, p. 513.

Russell makes two stabs at formulating the distinction. First, having stated the list of laws quoted in section 1 of this chapter, he writes:

> We may then say that *q* is *deducible* from *p* if it can be shown by means of the above principles that *p* implies *q*.

> This definition may be re-stated as follows. The laws of deduction tell us that two propositions having certain relations of form (e.g. that one is the negation of the negation of the other) are such that one of them implies the other. Thus *q* is deducible from *p* if *p* and *q* either have one of the relations contemplated by the laws of deduction, or are connected by any (finite) number of intermediaries each having one of these relations to its successor. (Ibid.)

We might put the point in proof-theoretic terms by saying that *q* is deducible from *p* if and only if a sentence expressing *q* can be obtained as the last line of a proof in an axiom system whose first line is a sentence expressing *p*. Russell ends with the observation that the definition captures the extension of the concept he is seeking to define:

> This meaning of *deducible* is purely logical, and covers, I think, exactly the cases in which, in practice, we can deduce a proposition *q* from a proposition *p* without assuming either that *p* is false or that *q* is true. (Ibid.)

Russell in effect offers a definition of the intuitive notion of deducibility in (proto) "proof-theoretic" terms. Russell is quite clear that he has only gestured towards the notion to be captured by the definition, but the notion of which he has a vague grasp looks very close to the notion of logical entailment.

With this definition in place Russell goes on to remark on the connection between deducibility and valid deductive inference. He writes:

> It is noteworthy that, in all actual valid deduction, whether or not the material is of a purely logical nature, the relation of premise to conclusion, in virtue of which we make the deduction, is one of those contemplated by the laws of logic or deducible from them. (Ibid., p. 517)

Russell's idea is that when an argument is valid, the corresponding material conditional is one that can be derived from "the laws of logic," by which Russell means the particular logical laws set out as the *axioms* of the system of the *Principles*.[204] It will be so derivable either because it is an instance of one of these general laws hence "contemplated by the law of logic"— or because it is derivable from several of them taken together.[205] For Russell, then, an argument is valid when and only when the truth of its corresponding material conditional is *grounded* in the logical laws that form the basis of a system of logic.

It is because both this view and Wittgenstein's own positive account can each be seen as explanations of what the notion of entailment consists in that I think it likely that in our key passage Wittgenstein is going against something like this view of Russell's. Unfortunately, however, this must remain something of a conjecture. We know that Wittgenstein cannot have heard this paper of Russell's because he was not anywhere near Oxford in 1905—in fact he was still at highschool. On the other hand, it is not unreasonable to suppose that Russell might have discussed the topic of the paper with Wittgenstein during the years 1911–1913, when the two philosophers got together, sometimes daily, to struggle with the philosophy of logic. At any rate, the view in question holds out some prospect of illuminating the key passage; and, given the lack of other plausible targets, I take that as an excellent reason to consider it in detail.

## [3] WITTGENSTEIN'S CRITIQUE

If this is the view Wittgenstein intended to oppose, what did he find objectionable in it? The objections are essentially those alluded to in the key passage. First, and most fundamentally, Russell's picture of validity rests on a faulty conception of the laws of logic as fact-presenting statements. For Wittgenstein, by contrast, there are no *laws* of logic and the so-called "logical truths," which Frege and Russell regard as instances of these laws, are merely sentences which, because they convey no information, are devoid of sense.

---

[204] Ibid., p. 516.
[205] Compare *CP Vol. IV*, p. 515. Notice that for Russell an implication holds between two propositions A and B when and only when A⊃B is true. Thus when A⊃B is false, implication is not said to relate these proposition, even though, Russell occasionally suggests, it is the relation of implication that provides unity to the propositional complex constituting this conditional, and so in some sense 'relates' the other propositional elements even when the conditional is false. (cf. *CP Vol. IV*, p. 380)

Consequently, far from expressing truths which lie at the bottom of all valid inferences, the laws of logic are to be viewed as expressing no facts of any kind. Secondly, even if Russell's conception of logic were correct, even if, that is to say, the laws of logic were not *sinnlos*, the appeal to logical laws in the explanation of valid inference would in any case be *superfluous*. As Wittgenstein sees the matter, if one proposition entails another, the entailment holds simply in virtue of the propositions' being the very propositions that they are.[206] There is no need to invoke any logical framework, as it were, holding premise and conclusion in place so that the relation of material implication obtaining between them may qualify *also* as a relation of entailment.[207] Something close to this thought is evident in the following remark from the *Tractatus*:

> If the truth of one proposition follows from the truth of others, this expresses itself in relations in which the forms[208] of these propositions stand to one another, and we do not need to put them in these relations first by connecting them with one another in a proposition; for these relations are internal, and exist as soon as, and by the very fact that, the propositions exist. (5.131)

As I read it, this passage is claiming that in order to appreciate that B follows from A there is no need first to show that the relation of material implication obtaining between these propositions in the

---

[206] The point is plausibly echoed in a remark from Wittgenstein's Cambridge lectures of 1931: "Propositions do not follow from one another as such; they simply are what they are" (*Lectures (1930–32)*, p. 57).

[207] To say that the recognition of logical inferential relations does not turn on the discernment of any worldly facts is not to embrace a conception of logic as somehow entirely without existential presuppositions, a free-floating entity having its nature quite independently of whether or not there is a world. As 5.5521 makes clear, such a conception would render mysterious how logic could apply to the world: "If logic were prior not just to how the world is but to the fact of its very existence how could we apply logic? We could say: if there were a logic, even if there were no world, how then could there be a logic, since there is a world?"

For Wittgenstein logic is simply a by-product of language designed to represent the world. If there were no world to be represented (whether truly or falsely) then there would be no logic either, because there would be no language. "The logical propositions describe the scaffolding of the world, or rather they present it. They "treat" of nothing. They presuppose that names have meaning, and that elementary propositions have sense. And this is their connection with the world." (6.124)

[208] To say there is a relation between the forms is to say that there is a relation between the propositions that holds in virtue of their forms.

further proposition "if A then B" is one that can be known to hold on the basis of the laws of logic alone. This is so because we do not need to think of the validity of the inference as owed to the logical truth of the corresponding conditional (nor, therefore, do we need to think of it as owed to the truth of the axioms from which the conditional may be proved).

Rather, what licenses the inference is nothing beyond the internal relatedness of the premise and conclusion themselves. This is something which is not to be dignified as a genuine fact but rather something that shows itself forth when we recognize the propositions for what they are. The attempt to give voice to what we recognize when we recognize this internal relatedness results in our saying things of the kind that Wittgenstein says at 5.11:

> If the truth-grounds which are common to a number of propositions are all also truth-grounds of some one proposition, we say that the truth of this proposition follows from the truth of those propositions.

But this talk of "truth-grounds" is not the statement of a model-theoretical conception of logical consequence. Rather, it has only an unofficial status as something meant to push us towards recognizing the internal relatedness of premises and conclusion. The unofficial talk of truth-grounds is something that guides our adoption of a particular perspicuous notation. (It makes clear what it is for a notation to count as perspicuous in the present connection.) Such a notation will be one where we can see in the signs something that notationally embodies the unofficial idea that every truth-ground of the conjunction of the premises is a truth-ground of the conclusion. The fact that no row of a sign of the truth-table notation for a valid a conditional has a "T" under the antecedent and an "F" under the consequent is one such notational embodiment.

The important point, however, is that propositions contain their own resources for revealing themselves to stand in the inferential relationships in which they stand. If *in practice* we sometimes need to derive a conditional in an axiom system in order to recognize the corresponding inference as valid, that is only because we are creatures with quite limited logical capacities. Axiom systems, which provide for what Wittgenstein calls proofs *in* logic— as opposed to proofs of one senseful proposition of the basis of one or more others—serve as no more than "mechanical aid[s] to the recognition of tautology in complicated cases" (6.1262) (my translation). Most importantly, they are not to be viewed as reflecting or recapitulating the structure of any supposed body of propositionally expressible "logical knowledge."

Wittgenstein's point against Russell and Frege is that the notion of derivability in a sound system cannot be invoked to explain the concept of entailment. The objection is *not* based on the worry that there might be valid arguments for which the relevant conditional is not derivable in the system. It is not, as we might put it today, the worry that the system may not be complete. Rather, it seems to be an objection of principle to the very idea that a relation as basic as entailment should be explicable in other terms.

There are in fact *three* objections that Wittgenstein might have in mind at this point. First, it could be claimed that Russell has the direction of explanation wrong. On the (tacit) assumption that Russell's system is deductively complete, it is the fact that A entails B that *explains* why the conditional "if A then B" is derivable, not the other way round. Secondly, on the proof-theoretic account of entailment one is encouraged to think of the axioms of the system as *primitively* logical and the conditionals derived from them as owing their logical truth to their being derivable from these axioms. Wittgenstein sees such a view as deeply flawed, and as encouraging the confused notion that self-evidence, which is a feature possessed by some logical laws but not by others, could be a mark of the primitively logical. It is such a view that Wittgenstein means to be opposing when he remarks that, on the contrary, "All propositions of logic are of equal rank; there are not some which are essentially primitive and others deduced from these" (6.127).[209] Thirdly, if we try to give a genuine reductive analysis of the notion of entailment, we risk making the facts of entailment seem to rest upon facts that are not, intuitively speaking, logical. From Wittgenstein's point of view, what Frege and Russell *call* the laws of logic are not intuitively logical laws at all. They are merely peculiarly compendious generalizations about what is actually the case,

---

[209] The whole quote is: "All propositions of logic are of equal rank; there are not some which are essentially primitive and others deduced from these. Every tautology itself shows that it is a tautology."

and this gives them the appearance of empirical laws, laws that is to say, whose negations we ought to be able to find intelligible.

## [4] A PROBLEM ABOUT UNDERSTANDING

In rejecting the idea that there is anything beyond the propositions themselves that grounds inferential transitions between propositions, Wittgenstein *can* seem to be blundering into a rather unattractive view. I have heard it claimed that, in taking our grasp of the inferential relations between propositions to depend on nothing beyond our understanding of the propositions themselves Wittgenstein commits himself to the plainly false view that we cannot grasp a proposition without thereby grasping all of its logical consequences. Now I do not myself think Wittgenstein is committed to such a view, but it is easy to see why someone might think he was. If the discernment of inferential relations between propositions does not require any very complicated proof, but depends only on our understanding of premise and conclusion, then it might seem that a failure to appreciate all of a proposition's consequences amounted to a failure fully to grasp the proposition itself. But since we do take ourselves to have a *full* grasp of many propositions, this may seem to imply that we must be fully apprised of *all* their logical consequences. But if that were so, then the capacity of deductive inference to *extend* our knowledge would itself seem to be called into question. I want to spend a moment discussing this issue, which is just a version of the question we identified as the seventh in our opening survey. I shall begin by saying a word about Dummett's proposed solution, which I take to be heading in the right direction, if not quite what is ultimately needed.

The problem is to explain how a deductive inference can both be recognizably justified, on the one hand, and capable of extending our knowledge, on the other. Dummett's solution is to appeal to our capacity to come to discern novel patterns in the sentences with which we are dealing in the course of following a proof. As Dummett points out, the sentence "Cato killed Cato," has something in common with the sentence "Cato killed Caesar," but also something (else) in common with the sentence "Brutus killed Brutus." What it has in common with the former sentence is that it instantiates the pattern expressed by the dyadic predicate '1 killed 2,' what it has in common with the latter is that it instantiates the pattern expressed by the monadic predicate '1 killed 1'. In order to understand the sentence "Cato killed Cato" we have to discern the first pattern in it, for it is essential to our grasp of this sentence that we can see it as expressing the holding of a dyadic relation. It's not, however, essential that we discern the second pattern in this sentence. Not, that is to say, until we wish to go on and draw the inference from "Cato killed Cato" to "Someone killed himself" For it is essential to our grasp of the quantified claim that we see it as the result of attaching an existential quantifier to the predicate '1 killed 1'. So in Dummett's view the reason why deductive argument can extend our knowledge is that it involves our seeing sentences as instantiating new patterns that we had not seen before.

In its proper place, Dummett's point is, I think, highly illuminating. Suppose we want to explain how logic—or as we should now say, not logic, but second order logic plus Hume's principle can "come to disgorge so rich a content"[210] as the Peano axioms. It is plausible that at least part of the explanation will advert to our ability to divine new patterns in our expressions. Certainly, as Jamie Tappenden has recently argued,[211] the use of definitions with a complex quantificational structure to coin new concepts, such as the concept of the ancestral of a relation, provides a large part of Frege's own answer to the question how logic comes to disgorge its rich content. And indeed, as was emphasized by George Boolos, it is possible to get contentful results, results of some mathematical power, using nothing besides second order logic and the definition of the ancestral (Frege's examples in *Begriffsschrift* being the transitivity and connectedness of the ancestral of an arbitrary single-valued relation).[212]

However, Dummett's solution, as he himself concedes, does not actually solve our *present* problem. For there exist inferences which plainly extend our knowledge but within which there is no recognition of new patterns, at least not, in the sense of coming to see the sentence we began with as containing the result of filling the argument places of a predicate we had not recognized in it before.

---

[210] *Grundlagen* § 16.
[211] Jamie Tappenden, "Extending Knowledge and 'Fruitful Concepts': Fregean Themes in the Foundations of Mathematics," *Noûs* vol. 29, No 4 (1995).
[212] *Begriffsschrift* propositions 98 and 133.

Consider, for example, the following valid argument from an introductory logic course:

Everyone loves a lover
Someone loves someone
Therefore,
Everyone loves everyone.

This simple argument has the power to delight us because its conclusion is so surprising. Yet when it is fully formalized in first order polyadic quantification theory it is plain that the only predicate discerned at any step is the *dyadic* predicate '1 loves 2'. The new insight seems to be injected into the argument by some means other than the recognition of new concepts.

True, in stating the argument we do analyse the predicate 'lover' in such a way as to reveal its hidden quantificational structure, so there is *one* place where we could argue that we have in some sense discerned a new pattern; but this cannot be the whole story, for the more clumsy formalized version of the argument is also surprising.

But if our having a capacity to come to discern new concepts in the course of a proof is not the general answer to the question how inference can be both justified and informative, then what is? Well, the first point to notice is that the solution need not be absolutely general. We may allow that *some* immediate inferences do not in fact extend our knowledge, so long as others do, and so long as some of these others figure in *all* arguments that we take to extend our knowledge. Also, we should bear in mind that it is not *altogether* obvious that an extension of our knowledge could only be achieved if there are some intermediate steps of the argument which by themselves extend our knowledge. After all, extension of knowledge is an intentional notion, and one lesson we ought to have learned from discussions of the intransitivity of indiscriminability is that discernible differences in such intentional notions as "how things appear to one" can sometimes be generated by stringing together sufficiently many subjectively indiscernible steps. That having been said, my solution will follow Dummett's in suggesting that there is an extension of knowledge over some individual *immediate* inferences.

I want to suggest that some extension of knowledge takes place even in the inference from, for example, "Fred loves someone" to "Someone loves someone". For, I claim, it is not true to say that we cannot recognize the truth of "Fred loves someone" without recognizing the truth of its existential generalization. What is true is that if I recognize the truth of the sentence "Fred loves someone" then I cannot but assent to the existential generalization "someone loves someone" *if* I'm confronted with the question whether or not it is true. Dummett is right to suggest that in recognizing the truth of the premises in a valid deductive argument I will have thereby recognized something that is sufficient for the truth of the conclusion, but in order to do so I need *not* have recognized this ground *as* sufficient for the conclusion, for I may not yet have *considered* the question whether it is sufficient. The step from premise to conclusion in a valid immediate deductive inference is a valid step because the grounds for the premise just are, among other things, grounds for the conclusion, but the step is nonetheless informative because it is not generally the case that in recognizing these grounds as grounds for the premise I need have recognized them as grounds for the conclusion. Of course, if the question is raised whether a conclusive ground for the premise in an immediate inference is also a conclusive ground for the conclusion, I will only be able to answer affirmatively, but that is because the property of the ground for the premises of being a ground for the conclusion will have then been rendered salient by the question's having been asked. The point is that the question need not have been rendered salient. Now, that said, I should admit that there are some inferences where simply grasping the premise as true requires me to recognize any grounds for the premise as grounds for the conclusion. We say that this is so, for example, in the case of an inference from a conjunction to one of its conjuncts. But the important point is that this is not, in general, the case.

These points may be illustrated by a consideration of the distinction between constructing and checking proofs. The reason proofs are compelling is that once the proof has been given, checking the steps is a simple mechanical process. We simply go through the steps of the proof and check that each one of them is covered by one or the other of the inference rules; and the inference rules are chosen to be such that they license only intuitively compelling transitions. What makes proofs *interesting*, of course, is that considerable ingenuity can be involved in constructing them. Skill in constructing proofs is a matter of knowing which questions to render salient at which points. Granted, the mathematically ignorant Meno can conduct a complex proof, but that is only because Socrates is there asking the right question at every step. It is Socrates who is really *proving* the theorem, for it is he, and only he, who knows which question to ask at each stage: Meno is no more than a proof-checker who is carried along by the persuasiveness of each of the individual steps.

## [5] ENTAILMENT AS AN INTERNAL RELATION

In the closing sections of this chapter I want to scrutinize more closely Wittgenstein's claim that the inference-licensing relation between the forms of the propositions is an *internal* one. What does Wittgenstein mean by "internal" in this context? Well, for Wittgenstein, a relation is internal if it is unthinkable that it should fail to relate its actual relata (4.123). For example, if this shade of blue is brighter than that shade, then it is unthinkable that these two shades should not be so related (4.123).

In presenting entailment as an internal relation, Wittgenstein is challenging Russell's view that all relations are external. Rebelling against the monistic idealism of F. H. Bradley, Russell writes in his 1899 essay "The Classification of Relations":

> Mr. Bradley has argued much and hotly against the view that relations are ever purely "external". I am not certain whether I understand what he means by this expression, but I think I should be retaining his phraseology if I described my view as the view that *all* relations are external. (*CP Vol. II*, p. 143)[213]

Russell's view, notice, is that he does not know what Bradley means, but he nonetheless regards it as wrong. Notice also how comprehensive is Russell's rejection of Bradley. He does not merely assert that *some* relations are external, which is all he needs to say in order to disagree with Bradley, he goes the whole hog and asserts the externality of all relations.[214]

---

[213] Given the date of this remark, it is worth mentioning that the bulk of the *Principles* appeared in the draft of May 1901, and that most of it was written during 1900. (See the Introduction to the 2nd Edition of the *Principles* p. v and *CP Vol. III*, 'Introduction' and 'Chronology'.)

[214] Now, because Russell may still be found speaking of the problems inherent in "the view that relations are not purely external" (*CP Vol. IV.*, p. 502) as late as 1905, it is plausible to suppose that he continued to subscribe to the contrary of Bradley's position throughout the period

*Continued on next page*

The view that all relations are external looks unpromising
if we understand externality in terms of Wittgenstein's notion
of "thinkability." For, we most naturally think of propositions
as incapable of standing in relations of entailment different
from those in which they actually stand. But it seems unlikely
that Russell would take himself to be committed to the externality of relations in *Wittgenstein's* sense. Rather, his intention
seems to be to claim that all relations are not-internal in whatever sense *Bradley* attaches to the term 'internal'. For Bradley a
relation is internal—or in his terminology 'intrinsical'—when it
"effects" or "passes into" or again, "penetrates the being of"
its terms.[215] Russell takes this to mean something very close to
what we should put today by saying that the relation super-
venes on the intrinsic features of its relata. In his essay "The
Monistic Theory of Truth" of 1906-7, Russell offers the following characterization of what it means to say that there are
external relations:

> There are such facts as that one object has a certain relation
> to another...[and such facts] do not imply that the two objects
> have...any *intrinsic* property distinguishing them from two
> objects which do not have the relation in question. (*PE*, p.
> 139–140)[216]

If we take "imply" here to mean "entail," we have something very
close to a denial of what we should today call a supervenience
claim. We might express Russell's idea as follows:

> A relation R is external (in the sense of not penetrating the
> being of its terms) just in case R *does not supervene* on the

---

1900–1905. Against this it should be mentioned that Russell does once
make a passing reference to internal relations in the *Principles* (§ 412).
However, it is far from clear that 'internality' in this context is supposed
to amount to Bradley's notion. (It may be that all he means is that a relation is 'internal' to a progression in the sense that a progression is ordered
by that relation, and so in a sense is built up out of it.)

[215] F. H. Bradley *Appearance and Reality: a Metaphysical Essay*, second
edition (Macmillan, 1908), p. 364.

[216] This chapter of *PE* is entitled "The Monistic Theory of Truth." The
material comprises the first two sections of a three-section paper that
Russell gave to the Aristotelian Society on December 3rd, 1906. The paper
was entitled "On The Nature of Truth." The editorial note *PE* p. 131
gives the incorrect title: "The Nature of Truth." (See "On the Nature of
Truth," *Proceedings of the Aristotelian Society* 1906–7, New Series—Vol.
7 (1907), pp. 28–49.)

intrinsic properties of its relata: That is to say just in case there are possible worlds w and w' and relata $X_1$, $Y_1$, $X_2$, $Y_2$ such that $X_1$ and $Y_1$ are in w and $X_2$ and $Y_2$ are in w' and neither the X's nor the Y's differ intrinsically, but where the relation relates only one of the pairs of relata.[217]

One might well have reservations about glossing the remark in this way, for the formulation I have given employs modal notions for which, officially, Russell has no time.[218] But, we should bear in mind that, in practice, Russell does not consistently maintain his antimodalist stance. He is prepared to invoke modal notions both in 1902 in speaking of logico-mathematical truths as governing "not only the actual world but every possible world"[219] and also in 1905 in characterizing, though not defining, propositions as *possible* objects of belief.[220] It does not seem outlandish, therefore, to suppose that Russell might have been employing modal notions—tacitly and unofficially—in trying to make sense of the idea that an internal relation "penetrates the being of its terms."

Let us suppose, then, that Russell's talk about externality is to be understood in terms of non-supervenience. Is this proposal compatible with his claim that *all* relations are external? I think not. Consider, for example, what it would be to assert the externality of the entailment relation. One would have to claim that there are two worlds w and w' and two pairs of propositions $<P_1,Q_1>$ and $<P_2,Q_2>$ such that the first pair is in w and the second in w' and where both the P's and the Q's agree in all their intrinsic properties, but where the members of only one pair stand related by entailment. But this is plainly false, for the relata in question, being propositions, are items for which a lack of intrin-

---

[217] We might be tempted to say: "just in case it is possible that $X_1$ and $Y_1$ should stand related by R and $X_2$ and $Y_2$ not do so, when neither the X's nor the Y's differ intrinsically," but the problem with this formulation is that it counts as internal relations which we would intuitively consider external. For the definition only considers pairs of relata contained in the same world. However, a relation which related one pair of items at one world, but failed to relate another intrinsically identical pair at another world is one we should intuitively wish to call external.

[218] The formulation also presupposes the availability of a workable distinction between intrinsic and relational properties; and that is a distinction that is notoriously hard to formulate. For a sense of the difficulties see David Lewis "Extrinsic Properties," *Philosophical Studies*, 44 (1983), pp. 197–200.

[219] See the 1902 paper "The Study of Mathematics" collected in *ML*, p. 55.

[220] See *CP Vol. IV*, p. 495.

sic difference amounts to a lack of numerical distinctness. If two propositions are to share all their intrinsic properties then they must contain exactly the same constituents, and must combine these constituents in the same way; but then they will just be the same propositions. And to suppose that the relation relates one-and-the-same pair of propositions in one world but not another is just to suppose it equally thinkable that the relation of entailment should both relate and not relate the propositions in question. But even Russell would not want to allow that a proposition can be conceived as having a range of *different* conceivable positions in the inferential network. So Russell must, in the end, deny that there are any such worlds as the ones we have tried to describe; and he must, accordingly, judge the relation of entailment internal.[221]

Faced with such a difficulty, a defender of Russell might of course reply that this only goes to show that I have misunderstood what it is for a relation to be internal in the sense of "penetrating the being of its terms." I think it is plausible, however, that *any* way of cashing this notion will run into similar problems (or worse). Consider, for example, the suggestion that the notion be fleshed out in terms of a counterfactual. We might try to say:

> A relation R is internal in the sense of penetrating the being of its terms *a* and *b* iff *a* and *b* would not be intrinsically exactly as they are, were they not so related.

In maintaining that *all* relations are external in the corresponding sense, we would commit ourselves to, among other things, asserting the following:

> It is not the case that: If the proposition *p and if p then q* were not to bear the relation of entailment to the proposition *q* then at least one of these propositions would be intrinsically altered.

---

[221] We might argue for the view that there cannot be two distinct propositions with the same intrinsic properties. Suppose there are two such. Then what renders them distinct must be their occupying distinct positions in a network of inferential relations. But that will not be possible without an intrinsic difference in the propositions. Intrinsically identical propositions must have the same inferential relations to other propositions (though the converse need not hold).

But the embedded counterfactual has an impossible antecedent, so, at least on one leading view of counterfactuals with impossible antecedents,[222] it will be vacuously true. But if so, then the whole statement in which the counterfactual is embedded will be vacuously false. Hence, entailment will turn out not to be an external relation after all, and Russell's claim that all relations are external will therefore be false.

These reflections feed the suspicion that we will be unable to explain Russell's notion of an external relation in a way that is compatible with the doctrine that *all* relations are external. Of course, this suspicion can only be confirmed in a piecemeal fashion by examining individual proposals for cashing the notion of 'externality' as they arise. But it is not Wittgenstein's business in the *Tractatus* to run through all the ways one might try to cash the notion of an external relation. His aim is to issue a challenge to Russell to come up with a sense for the notion of an external relation that obeys the constraints Russell tries to impose on it. The *prima facie* unsuitability of Wittgenstein's own characterization of externality in terms of thinkability is just part of this challenge. Russell will clearly refuse Wittgenstein's characterization, but then it will be up to him to say what he means by "external."

## [6] METHODOLOGICAL CONSIDERATIONS

I take this discussion to have illustrated a quite general point about the philosophical method of the *Tractatus*. I take it to show that there is a sense in which some of the most important business of the *Tractatus* takes place off the page. Wittgenstein notoriously concludes the *Tractatus* by adjudging its claims nonsense. We can come to understand why Wittgenstein should nonetheless have written such a book if we recognize his own apparently categorical pronouncements as utterances having only the *surface-form* of disagreements with the views of Russell and Frege. Wittgenstein does not himself regard these disagreements as substantial, for he sees both parties as having failed to attach meaning to at least some of the crucial terms employed in the debate.[223] His purpose is not to persuade Russell or Frege of any positive doctrines, but to

---

[222] David Lewis, *Counterfactuals* (Oxford: Blackwell, 1973), § 1.6, pp. 24–6.
[223] Wittgenstein himself has not gone on to cash out the notion of "thinkability."

get them to see for themselves that their theoretical notions cannot bear the weight that their positive doctrines place upon them. In our example, Russell must come to see that there is no sense to the notion of an external relation that is compatible with the externality of *all* relations.

Much of the *Tractatus'* value as a philosophical work lies in its power to *provoke* the kind of dialectic we have just rehearsed in the case of the relation of externality. However, it is important to acknowledge that this dialectic is not *explicitly* presented in the book's pages. Rather, Wittgenstein sees the need to make provocative categorical pronouncements in the *Tractatus* as a necessary evil, one which would be avoided in a more ideal philosophical setting. This thought, I would argue, explains the subjunctive conditionals in the passage near the close of the *Tractatus* where Wittgenstein outlines what *would* ideally be the correct method in philosophy. Wittgenstein says:

> The right method of philosophy would actually be this. To say nothing except what can be said, that is, the propositions of natural science, that is, something that has nothing to do with philosophy: and then always, when someone else wished to say something metaphysical, to demonstrate to him that he had given no meaning to certain signs in his propositions. This method would be unsatisfying to the other—he would not have the feeling that we were teaching him philosophy— but it would be the only strictly correct method. (6.53)

Now the *Tractatus*, plainly, does not embody this method, for it contains few sentences that state propositions of natural science. It does, however, anticipate the debunking part of the "strictly correct" method, in its capacity to bring its readers to the realization that they have attached no meaning to certain of their philosophical terms. I have illustrated how this is so with reference only to the notions of "internal" and "external" relations. A fully adequate reading of the *Tractatus* would need to make a parallel case for many other key philosophical concepts, such as "proposition," "object," "propositional function," and the like. I have not made such a case, but I do hope in this chapter to have illustrated an approach to reading Wittgenstein's early philosophy that will allow us to retain certain critical insights, while respecting the *Tractatus's* closing strictures.

# Appendix

Consider the following two consecutive remarks from the *Tractatus*:

> In order to understand the essence of the proposition, consider hieroglyphic writing, which pictures the facts it describes.
>     And from it came the alphabet without the essence of the representation being lost. (4.016)

> This we see from the fact that we understand the sense of the propositional sign, without having had it explained to us. (4.02)

*What* are we supposed to see from the fact that we understand the propositional sign without having had it explained to us? That hieroglyphic writing pictures the facts it describes? Surely not! That the alphabet came from hieroglyphic writing without the essence of the representation being lost? If there is a connection, it is not obvious. But rather than strain to make out a connection I suggest we look elsewhere for the referent of "this". If we remember the manner of composition of the *Tractatus*: that it was composed by rearranging already drafted passages from the *Prototractatus*, it becomes a possible hypothesis that 4.02 was lifted from an earlier context where the 'this' referred not to 4.016 but to something in another passage. An examination of the *Prototractatus* supports this idea.

In the *Prototractatus*, *Tractatus* 4.02 occurs as *PT* 4.02 on page 8 of the manuscript, while *Tractatus* 4.016 occurs as *PT*

4.0115—4.0116 on page 26 of the manuscript. So at the time of writing *PT* 4.02, the word 'this' cannot have referred to *Tractatus* 4.016, for it simply hadn't at that point been written down in the *Prototractatus*. What, then, is the antecedent of 'this' in *Tractatus* 4.02? Here the matter is complicated by Wittgenstein's clearly having re-numbered some of the passages in the *Prototractatus*. The relevant stretch of the *Prototractatus* reads as follows:

| | |
|---|---|
| 4.01 | A proposition is a picture of reality. |
| 4.08 | Reality is compared with a proposition. |
| 4.09 | A proposition can only be true or false by being a picture of reality. |
| 4.02 | This we see from the fact that we understand the sense of the propositional sign without having had it explained to us. |
| 4.03 | The meanings of the simple signs, words, must be explained to us, if we are to understand them. |
| 4.04 | With propositions, however, we make ourselves understood. |
| 4.05 | It belongs to the essence of a proposition that is should be able to communicate to us a sense which is *new to us*?[224] |
| 4.06 | A proposition communicates a situation to us, and so it must be *essentially* connected with that situation. |
| 4.07 | And the connexion is precisely that it is its logical picture. |
| 3.141 | A simple sign means an object. The object is its meaning. |

It seems that originally the second and third lines quoted (i.e. 4.08 and 4.09) were part of one remark—perhaps 4.01, or perhaps a separately numbered remark beginning with the second line (it doesn't matter which).[225] It appears that some time after completing the series of remarks culminating in 4.07 Wittgenstein must

---

[224] The question mark attaches not to the whole remark but only to the interpolated 'to us', which Wittgenstein decided to include in the *Tractatus*.

[225] The '8' is in darker pencil than the '4.0' and appears to be written over another numeral, perhaps '2'. '4.09' doesn't seem to be written over any numeral.

have returned to this part of his manuscript and renumbered the second and third lines as "4.08" and "4.09," respectively. One reason he may have wished to do this is simply to make it clear that the 'this' in 4.02 is intended to refer to the first line rather than to the second or third (though he may have had other reasons). What is important is that in the *Prototractatus* the 'this' in 4.02 is intended to refer to 4.01.[226] It seems that in rearranging the remarks for the *Tractatus* Wittgenstein inserted a whole block of text between PT 4.01 and PT 4.02—viz. the one stretching from *Tractatus* 4.011 to *Tractatus* 4.016. When he did so he must have forgotten that it was important to keep 4.02 as the immediate successor of 4.01. It would have been easy to make this mistake because the numbering system of the *Prototractatus* does not encode information about relations of *immediate* succession. (2.02 for example, may not end up occurring immediately after 2.01, for 2.011 might intervene.)

So the long and short of the matter is that the 'this' of *Tractatus* 4.02 is supposed to refer to *Tractatus* 4.01. Consequently, the ground for saying that the proposition is a picture—or "a model of the reality as we know it"—is that we can understand the sense of a propositional sign without having had it explained to us.

---

[226] PT 4.08 ends up as *Tractatus* 4.05.

# Bibliography

## WORKS BY WITTGENSTEIN

*Notebooks, 1914–1916*, edited by G. H. von Wright and G. E. M. Anscombe, trans. G. E. M. Anscombe (Oxford: Blackwell, 1961).

*Prototractatus: An early version of Tractatus Logico-Philosophicus by Ludwig Wittgenstein*, B. F. McGuinness, T. Nyberg, and G. H. von Wright, eds. (London: Routledge and Kegan Paul Ltd., 1971).

*Ludwig Wittgenstein Logisch-Philosophische Abhandlung: kritische Edition*, B. McGuinness and J. Schulte eds. (Frankfurt am Main: Suhrkamp, 1989).

*Tractatus Logico-Philosophicus*, trans. C. K. Ogden (London: Routledge and Kegan Paul Ltd, 1922).

*Tractatus Logico-Philosophicus*, trans. D. F. Pears and B. McGuinness (London: Routledge and Kegan Paul Ltd., 1961).

*Ludwig Wittgenstein Cambridge Letters: Correspondence with Russell, Keynes, Moore, Ramsey and Sraffa*, B. McGuinness & G. H. von Wright, eds. (Oxford: Blackwell, 1995).

*Letters to C.K. Ogden with comments on the English Translation of the Tractatus Logico-Philosophicus*, G.H. von Wright, ed. (Oxford: Blackwell/RKP, 1973).

*Philosophical Grammar*, R Rhees, ed., trans. A Kenny (Oxford: Basil Blackwell, 1974).

*Wittgenstein's Lectures Cambridge, 1930–32, From the notes of John King and Desmond Lee*, Desmond Lee, ed., first published 1980, Midway Reprint (Chicago: University of Chicago Press, 1989).

*Wittgenstein's Lectures Cambridge, 1932–35, From the Notes of Alice Ambrose and Margaret MacDonald*, Alice Ambrose, ed., first published 1979, Midway reprint (Chicago: University of Chicago Press, 1989).

*Philosophical Investigations* trans. G. E. M. Anscombe (New York: Macmillan, 1953).

## WORKS BY RUSSELL

*Philosophical Papers 1896–99, The Collected Papers of Bertrand Russell, Vol. II*, Edited by Nicholas Griffin, Albert C. Lewis, and William C. Stratton (London: Routledge, 1990).

*The Philosophy of Leibniz*, first published 1900, reprinted (London: Routledge, 1992).

*Toward the "Principles of Mathematics," 1900–02, The Collected Papers of Bertrand Russell, Vol. III*, Gregory H. Moore, ed. (London: Routledge, 1993).

*The Principles of Mathematics* (London: Allen & Unwin, 1903).

*Foundations of Logic 1903–05, The Collected Papers of Bertrand Russell, Vol. IV*, edited by Alasdair Urquhart with the assistance of Albert C. Lewis (London: Routledge, 1994).

"On the Nature of Truth," *Proceedings of the Aristotelian Society* 1906–7, New Series Vol. 7 (1907), pp. 28–49.

*Philosophical Essays*, first published 1910 (London: Routledge, 1994).

*Principia Mathematica* to \*56, with A.N. Whitehead, first published 1910–13 (Cambridge: Cambridge University Press, 1990).

*The Problems of Philosophy*, first published 1912 (Oxford: Oxford University Press, 1986).

*Mysticism and Logic*, first published 1917 (Totowa, New Jersey: Barnes and Noble, 1981).

*Introduction to Mathematical Philosophy*, first published 1919, reprinted with an introduction by J. G. Slater (London: Routledge, 1993).

*My Philosophical Development*, first published 1959 (London: Routledge, 1993).

## WORKS BY FREGE

*Begriffsschrift, eine der arithmetischen nachgebildete Formelsprache des reinen Denkens* (Halle: Louis Nebert, 1879). (English translation in van Heijenoort (1967)).

*Grundlagen: Die Grundlagen der Arithmetik,* first published as *Die Grundlagen der Arithmetik: eine logisch-mathematische Untersuchung über den Begriff der Zahl,* first published 1884, Christian Thiel, ed. (Hamburg: Meiner, 1986).

*Funktion, Begriff, Bedeutung. Fünf logische Studien,* Günther Patzig, ed., second edition (Göttingen, 1966).

*Grundgesetze der Arithmetik,* first published 1893 part I, 1903 part II (Hildesheim: Olms, 1962); *The Basic Laws of*

*Arithmetic*, trans. and ed., M. Furth (English translation of Introduction and first 52 sections) (Berkeley and Los Angeles: University of California Press, 1964).

*Collected Papers*, Brian McGuinness, ed., trans. Hans Kaal et. al. (Oxford: Blackwell, 1980).

*Gottlob Frege Posthumous Writings*, Hans Hermes, Friedrich Kambartel and Friedrich Kaulbach, eds., trans. Peter Long and Roger White (Oxford: Blackwell, 1980).

## WORKS BY OTHER AUTHORS

Anscombe, G. E. M. *An Introduction to Wittgenstein's Tractatus.* (Philadelphia: University of Pennsylvania Press, 1959).

Austin, J. L. *Philosophical Papers*, third edition, first published 1961 (Oxford: Oxford University Press, 1979).

Baker, G. *Wittgenstein, Frege and the Vienna Circle* (Oxford: Blackwell, 1988).

Black, M. *A Companion to Wittgenstein's 'Tractatus'* (Ithaca: Cornell, 1964).

Boolos, G. "Reading the *Begriffsschrift*," *Mind*, Vol. XCIV, no. 375 (1985), pp. 331–344.

Bradley, F. H. *Appearance and Reality: a Metaphysical Essay*, first published 1893, second edition (Oxford: Clarendon Press, 1968).

Brockhaus, R. G. *Pulling up the Ladder: The Metaphysical Roots of Wittgenstein's Tractatus Logico-Philosophicus* (La Salle, Illinois: Open Court, 1991).

Carroll, L. "What the Tortoise said to Achilles," *Mind* 4 (1895), pp. 278–80.

Carruthers, P. *Tractarian Semantics: Finding sense in Wittgenstein's Tractatus* (Oxford: Blackwell, 1989).

Cartwright, R. *Philosophical Essays* (Cambridge Mass.: MIT Press, 1987).

Chomsky, N. *Aspects of the Theory of Syntax* (Cambridge Mass.: MIT Press, 1965).

Diamond, C. *The Realistic Spirit: Wittgenstein, Philosophy and the Mind* (Cambridge, Mass.: MIT Press, 1991).

Dreben, B. & Floyd, J. "Tautology: How not to use a word," *Synthese* 87, 1991, pp. 23–49.

Dummett, M. "Frege and Wittgenstein" in I. Block, ed. *Perspectives on the Philosophy of Wittgenstein* (Cambridge Mass.: MIT. Press, 1981).

———. *Frege, Philosophy of Language*, second edition, (London: Duckworth, 1981).

———. *Frege, Philosophy of Mathematics* (Cambridge, Mass.: Harvard University Press, 1991)

———. *The Logical Basis of Metaphysics* (Cambridge, Mass.: Harvard University Press, 1991).

Favrholdt, D. *An Interpretation and Critique of Wittgenstein's Tractatus* (Copenhagen: Munksgaard, 1964).

Fogelin, R. J. *Wittgenstein*, second edition (Routledge & Kegan Paul Ltd., 1987).

Geach, P. T. "Saying and Showing in Frege and Wittgenstein," in *Essays in Honour of G. H. von Wright*, J. Hintikka ed., *Acta Philosophica Fennica 28* (Amsterdam, 1976).

Goldfarb, W. "Logic in the Twenties: the Nature of the Quantifier" *Journal of Symbolic Logic* 44 (1979), pp. 351-68.

————. "Metaphysics and Nonsense: on Cora Diamond's *The Realistic Spirit*," *Journal of Philosophical Research*, volume 22 (1997), pp. 57–73.

————. "Frege's Conception of Logic" forthcoming in J. Floyd and S. Shieh, eds., *Futures Past: Reflections on the History and Nature of Analytic Philosophy* (Harvard University Press).

Griffin, J. *Wittgenstein's Logical Atomism* (Oxford: Oxford University Press, 1964).

Heck, R. "Frege and Semantics," forthcoming in T. Ricketts, ed., *The Cambridge Companion to Frege*.

Harman, G. *Change in View: Principles of Reasoning* (Cambridge, Mass.: MIT Press, 1986).

Hintikka, J., ed., *Essays in Honour of G.H. von Wright, Acta Philosophical Fennica 28* (Amsterdam, 1976).

Husserl, E. *Logische Untersuchungen*, first published 1900–1901; second revised edition (Halle: Niemeyer, 1913–1920).

Hylton, P. *Russell, Idealism and the Emergence of Analytic Philosophy* (Oxford: Oxford University Press, 1990).

————. "Functions, Operations and Sense in Wittgenstein's *Tractatus*" in Tait (1997).

Kant, I. *Kritik der reinen Vernunft*—trans. by Norman Kemp Smith as *Immanuel Kant's Critique of Pure Reason* (London: Macmillan, 1929).

Kenny, A. *Wittgenstein*, first published 1973 (Harmondsworth: Penguin Books Ltd., 1986)

Lewis, D. "Extrinsic Properties," *Philosophical Studies* 44 (1983), pp. 197–200.

———. *Counterfactuals* (Oxford: Blackwell, 1973).

———. *On the Plurality of Worlds* (Oxford: Blackwell, 1987).

Mayer, V. "The Numbering System of the *Tractatus*," *Ratio* (New Series) VI, December (1993), pp. 108–119.

McGuinness, B. *Wittgenstein, a life: Young Ludwig* (1889–1921), first published by Gerald Duckworth & Co., 1988 (London: Penguin, 1990).

———. "Wittgenstein's pre-*Tractatus* manuscripts" in *Grazer Philosophische Studien* 33 (1989), pp. 35–47.

Mounce, H. O. *Wittgenstein's Tractatus* (Oxford, Blackwell, 1981).

Pears, D. *The False Prison, A Study in the Development of Wittgenstein's Philosophy, Volume One* (Oxford: Oxford University Press, 1987).

Quine, W. V. *From a Logical Point of View* (Cambridge, Mass.: Harvard University Press, 1943).

———. *Word and Object* (Cambridge, Mass.: M.I.T. Press, 1960).

Ricketts, T. "Objectivity and Objecthood: Frege's Metaphysics of Judgement" in *Frege Synthesized*, Leila Haaparanta and Jaakko Hintikka, eds. (Dortrecht, 1986).

———. "Frege, the *Tractatus*, and the Logocentric Predicament," *Noûs* (1985), pp. 3–15.

———. *The Theory of Types and the Limits of Sense* (unpublished typescript).

———. "Pictures, logic, and the limits of sense in Wittgenstein's *Tractatus*," in Sluga and Stern (1996), pp. 59–99.

Sluga, H. and D. G. Stern, eds., *The Cambridge Companion to Wittgenstein* (Cambridge: Cambridge University Press, 1996).

Stenius, E. *Wittgenstein's Tractatus: A critical exposition of its main lines of thought* (Ithaca: Cornell University Press, 1964).

Sullivan, P. "A Version of the Picture Theory," in W. Vossenkuhl, ed., *Wittgenstein: Tractatus* (Akademie Verlag, 1997).

Tait, W., ed., *Early Analytic Philosophy: Frege, Russell, Wittgenstein Essays in Honor of Leonard Linsky* (Chicago and La Salle, Illinois: Open Court, 1997).

Tappenden, J. "Extending Knowledge and 'Fruitful Concepts': Fregean Themes in the Foundations of Mathematics," *Noûs* vol. 29, No 4 (1995).

van Heijenoort, J. *From Frege to Gödel: A Source Book in Mathematical Logic, 1879–1931* (Cambridge, Mass.: Harvard University Press, 1967).

———. "Logic as Calculus and Logic as Language," *Synthese* 17 (1967), pp. 324–330.

# Index